The first United States Olympic delegation poses in the
stadium in Athens, 1896. Following pages: The crowd cheers as
the torch is borne into the arena in Barcelona, 1992.

IOC Olympic Museum Collections

Cover, clockwise from top left:

Buddy Davis, Helsinki, 1952 HULTON ARCHIVE/GETTY IMAGES Greg Louganis, Seoul, 1988 NEIL LEIFER
Ray Ewry, St. Louis, 1904 BROWN BROTHERS Mia Hamm, Atlanta, 1996 CHRIS COLE/DUOMO/CORBIS
Jesse Owens, Berlin, 1936 AP WIDE WORLD Olga Korbut, Munich, 1972 JOHN DOMINIS
Bob Mathias, London, 1948 ALPHA/EMPICS Carl Lewis, Los Angeles, 1984 RICH CLARKSON/SPORTS ILLUSTRATED

LIFE

The Olympics

From Athens to Athens

**An Illustrated History
of the Summer Games**

LIFE

Editor Robert Sullivan
Creative Director
Ian Denning
Picture Editor
Barbara Baker Burrows
Executive Editor
Robert Andreas
Associate Picture Editor
Christina Lieberman
Senior Reporter
Hildegard Anderson
Copy JC Choi (Chief),
Mimi McGrath,
Wendy Williams
Production Manager
Michael Roseman
Picture Research
Rachel Hendrick
Photo Assistant
Joshua Colow

Publisher Andrew Blau
Finance Director
Craig Ettinger
Assistant Finance Manager
Karen Tortora

Editorial Operations
Richard K. Prue (Director),
Richard Shaffer (Manager),
Brian Fellows, Raphael Joa,
Stanley E. Moyse
(Supervisors), Keith Aurelio,
Gregg Baker, Charlotte Coco,
Scott Dvorin, Kevin Hart,
Rosalie Khan, Po Fung Ng,
Barry Pribula, David Spatz,
Vaune Trachtman, Sara
Wasilausky, David Weiner

Time Inc. Home Entertainment
President Rob Gursha
Vice President, Branded Businesses
David Arfine
Vice President, New Product Development Richard Fraiman
Executive Director, Marketing Services Carol Pittard
Director, Retail & Special Sales
Tom Mifsud
Director of Finance Tricia Griffin
Assistant Marketing Director
Ann Marie Doherty
Prepress Manager Emily Rabin
Book Production Manager
Jonathan Polsky
Associate Product Manager
Jennifer Dowell

Special thanks to Bozena Bannett,
Alexandra Bliss, Bernadette Corbie,
Robert Dente, Gina Di Meglio,
Anne-Michelle Gallero, Peter Harper,
Suzanne Janso, Robert Marasco,
Natalie McCrea, Margarita Quiogue,
Mary Jane Rigoroso, Steven
Sandonato, Grace Sullivan

Published by

LIFE Books

Time Inc.
1271 Avenue of the Americas,
New York, NY 10020

ISBN: 1-932273-62-x
Library of Congress Control Number:
2004105402

Mark Spitz pulls away from the field and shatters the world record in the 200-meter butterfly for the first of his seven gold medals at the 1972 Munich Olympics.

We welcome your comments and
suggestions about LIFE Books. Please
write to us at: LIFE Books, Attention:
Book Editors, PO Box 11016,
Des Moines, IA 50336-1016

If you would like to order any of our
hardcover Collector's Edition books,
please call us at 1-800-327-6388
(Monday through Friday, 7:00 a.m.–
8:00 p.m. or Saturday, 7:00 a.m.–6:00
p.m. Central Time).

Please visit us, and sample past
editions of LIFE, at www.LIFE.com.

Iconic images from the LIFE Picture
Collection are now available as fine art
prints and posters. The prints are
reproductions on archival, resin-coated
photographic paper, framed in black
wood, with an acid-free mat. Works by
the famous LIFE photographers—
Eisenstaedt, Parks, Bourke-White,
Burrows, among many others—are
available. The LIFE poster collection
presents large-format, affordable,
suitable-for-framing images. For more
information on the prints, priced at
$99 each, call 888-933-8873 or go to
www.purchaseprints.com. The posters
may be viewed and ordered at
www.LIFEposters.com.

Co Rentmeester

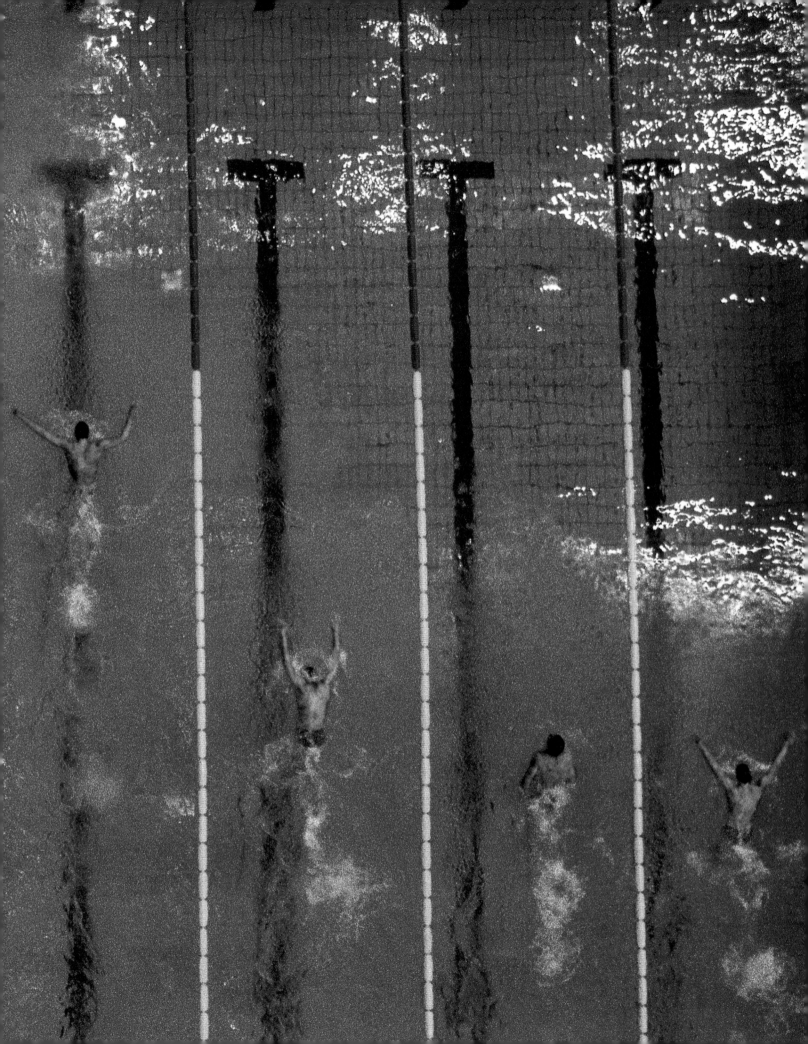

The Resilient Olympic Spirit

Frank Shorter wins the marathon at the 1972 Olympic Games in Munich. He has stayed involved in athletics since his Olympic career ended in 1976, and recently has been vocal in the fight against performance-enhancing drugs.

Baron Pierre de Coubertin, the French pedagogue and historian, could never have envisioned the legacy that would be spawned by his inspiration to resurrect the ancient Olympic Games in Athens in 1896. All that this nobleman did know was some of the myth and history of the Games of ancient Greece, where, during the time set aside for athletic competition, a universal truce was declared, and mankind's penchant for war and hostility subsided for a brief moment. But that's all that de Coubertin needed to know. That was the spirit of the past he was hoping to rekindle: man's inhumanity to man suspended while athletic performance, devoid of politics, could be witnessed, appreciated and rewarded.

I doubt he could ever have imagined how the Games of the Modern Olympics would evolve into a worldwide sporting event of such physical, financial and social magnitude as we see today. In the 21st century, the whole of the Olympics is indeed much more than the sum of its parts—these parts being the athletes themselves.

There was a long Olympic era when these sportsmen and women were mainly those who could afford the time to train and travel. American athletes in the 1920s and 1930s drank champagne while taking steamships to the Games in Europe. Much of the rest of the world could not afford to play. Universality was to come later.

Maybe it took two world wars for our planet to appreciate how much it needed the Olympics. After the War to End All Wars and then World War II, there was a yearning in many places for commonality, even as other countries descended into a cold war. The Olympic spectacle as we now know it began to take on recognizable form in the 1956 Olympics in Melbourne. The world, perhaps sensing an increasing importance in marching into a stadium behind the interlocking rings of the Olympic flag, made the effort to get to Australia, and to experience not only the events but also the country. Nationhood began to rise as an element in the Olympics: Democracy and communism began to be associated with athletic achievement.

Around the world, people were buying more televisions, and the Olympics made for a perfect television spectacle. Olympic champions were on their way to becoming household names. Others, some with sinister motives, took note of the Games' exploding growth—and directly violated the unspoken truce.

Many consider the 1972 Olympics in Munich to be a turning point in the history of the Games. Television had truly come of age, and now had an ability to create a world stage. Terrorism could not resist the temptation to walk to the center. The massacre of the Israeli athletes reminded all of us who were in the Olympic Village at the time that the sanctuary of the Games was fragile, if also very much worth supporting with our sweat and emotion. At first, my friends and I wanted to go home—nothing was worth a human life, not even competing in the Olympics. But we stayed, and history has shown us that we were right to do so.

The United States did not go to the 1980 Olympic Games in Moscow for a reason remembered by some but not many of its citizens, and the Eastern Bloc countries returned the favor in 1984, boycotting Los Angeles for equally forgettable reasons. Throughout it all, the athletes who did attend continued to compete on the levelest of playing fields, setting their records and reminding all of us that there are times when athletes can focus and approach purity of effort, no matter the distraction.

Now the Games will return to Athens and perhaps another turning point. The expense of putting

on, and the worldwide attention paid to, the Olympic Games, are at all-time highs. Security has never been tighter, and the potential rewards to both the winning athletes and their countries have never been greater. I am curious to see what transpires between the Opening and Closing ceremonies in the Olympic Stadium this summer. Whatever it is, the Olympic Games will endure.

Plus ça change, plus il rest la même chose. ("The more it changes, the more it stays the same.") Since de Coubertin, a Frenchman, founded the Modern Games, I like the fact that this French expression well describes the perpetual resilience—and hope—that I continue to see in the Olympic Games, and in the athletes who compose its intangible spirit. The aspiration of the athlete, and the drama of compe-

tition, are irresistible. There are few moments in any lifetime when one can feel that, for an instant, he or she is the best in the world at something. The event may seem odd, the distance arbitrary; after all, why is the Olympic marathon 26.2 miles long? Regardless: Just for an instant, the athlete on the top step of the podium receiving a gold medal can feel that competitors from the entire world were there on that day, vying for that spot, and that he or she is the lucky one. This is a feeling I wish every athlete could experience, and the essence of the goal and its pursuit has not changed, nor will it.

The images of Olympics before my time allowed me to dream of being there. The images that have been forged after remind me of the timeless and uncontrollable nature of the Olympic Spirit.

Spiridon Louis of Greece (in traditional white garb) was the winner of the first marathon. During the Olympic festivities in 1896, he and Greek princes George and Nicholas host an outing in the woods for athletes from several nations.

1896 Athens *Page 10*

1900 Paris *Page 14*

1904 St. Louis *Page 18*

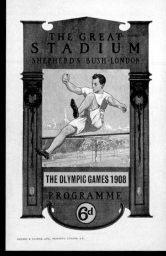

1908 London *Page 22*

1896, 1908: IOC Olympic Museum Collections;
1900: The Granger Collection, New York;
1904: IOC Olympic Museum/Allsport/Getty Images

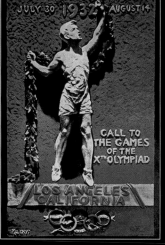

1932 Los Angeles *Page 46*

1936 Berlin *Page 52*

1948 London *Page 58*

1952 Helsinki *Page 64*

1932, 1952: IOC Olympic Museum/Allsport/
Getty Images; 1936, 1948: IOC Olympic Museum Collections

1972 Munich *Page 94*

1976 Montreal *Page 100*

1980 Moscow *Page 106*

1984 Los Angeles *Page 112*

IOC Olympic Museum/Allsport/Getty Images (4)

1912 Stockholm *Page 28*   **1920 Antwerp** *Page 32*   **1924 Paris** *Page 36*   **1928 Amsterdam** *Page 40*

1956 Melbourne *Page 70*   **1960 Rome** *Page 76*   **1964 Tokyo** *Page 82*   **1968 Mexico City** *Page 88*

1988 Seoul *Page 118*   **1992 Barcelona** *Page 124*   **1996 Atlanta** *Page 130*   **2000 Sydney** *Page 136*

1896 *Athens*

March 25 to April 3
311 men, **13** countries
Greece **47** medals (**10** firsts)
U.S.A. **19** medals (**11** firsts)
Cost **3,740,000** drachmas ($542,300)

The first modern Olympic Games were athletically unimpressive (not one world record was set), yet by every other standard— aesthetics, organization, attendance (40,000 watched the swimming events)—they were a great success. This was the result of hard work by hundreds of Greeks, not least King George himself. The monarch helped squeeze the financing from a reluctant public—including a million drachmas from commodities merchant George Averoff to build the magnificent white marble stadium.

Unfortunately for Olympics advocate Baron Pierre de Coubertin, as the Games drew closer, Averoff became more and more the center of attention, and adulation. The Greek citizenry erected a marble statue of Averoff outside the stadium and praised his name to the skies. In contrast, the baron's name appeared nowhere in official literature. When de Coubertin tried to wring out some credit by declaring, "I hereby assert once more my claims for being sole author of the whole project," an Athens newspaper labeled him "a thief seeking to rob Greece of her inheritance."

Eventually, Greece joined the rest of the world in embracing de Coubertin as the true originator of the modern Olympics. In addition, he was also a competitor of sorts, winning a gold medal in the cultural competition at the 1912 Stockholm Games for a poem he wrote under a German pseudonym.

Though de Coubertin had started one of the 20th century's most important and popular movements, he seemed to draw little pleasure from it in his advancing years. He didn't attend any Games after 1924; by the '30s, his family fortune gone, he lived in Switzerland with his wife and a mentally disturbed daughter in a hotel suite donated by the municipality of Lausanne. European friends nominated him for the Nobel Peace Prize in 1936, but the jury chose an Argentinian lawyer instead. He died of a stroke the following year at the age of 74.

Baron Pierre de Coubertin

Brown Brothers; left inset: IOC Olympic Museum Collections; right inset: Polaris

At right, the Acropolis towers over the statue of George Averoff at the entrance to the Olympic stadium.

Bostonian **Thomas Burke** (second from left) assumes the revolutionary "crouch" start. Burke won this event, the 100 meters, as well as the 400. Top right: Fittingly, a Greek, **Spiridon Louis**, won the marathon, a race in emulation of ancient Philippides' fabled run from Marathon to Athens. Below, French cyclists **Paul Masson** (left) and **Léon Flameng** won four races between them.

Ivy League champs: **Robert Garrett**, a 20-year-old Princetonian, was introduced to the discus by a history professor and won the event in Athens. **James Connolly**, a 27-year-old Harvard undergraduate, was denied a leave of absence by the dean, so he dropped out of school to compete in the triple jump, which opened the Games. Connolly won, and thus became the first Olympic champion since Armenian boxer Prince Varasdates in 369 A.D.

Albert Meyer/IOC Olympic Museum Collections; inset: Allison Archives First Olympic Collection

July 2 to July 22
1,319 men, **11** women, **22** countries
France **102** medals (**29** firsts)
U.S.A. **53** medals (**20** firsts)

Staged as an amusing sidelight to the World's Fair, the 1900 Games had no Opening Ceremony and few spectators. The word "Olympic" never appeared in the official program, and many competitors returned home unaware they had even been in an Olympic Games. The IOC didn't decide until it was all over exactly which events would be recognized. Croquet, golf, cricket and tug-of-war were included. Fishing in the Seine, pigeon-flying and fire-extinguishing were not.

Because women were allowed to compete, Margaret Abbott, 22, a five-foot-eleven Chicago socialite studying art in Paris, entered the nine-hole golf event, which was called at the time by *Golf Illustrated,* "The International Golf Competition at Compiegne in connection with the Paris Exhibition," and judged a "fashionable and successful gathering." Margaret Abbott finished first with a 47 in a field that included her mother, the noted novelist and editor Mary Ives Abbott. Mom shot a 65.

Modestly, Margaret said that her victory came mainly because her French competitors "misunderstood the nature of the game and turned up to play in high heels and tight skirts." She never got a medal and, so, never knew she was America's first female Olympic champion. By taking the tennis title a few days earlier, Britain's Charlotte Cooper became the first woman to win any event.

During her Paris sojourn, Abbott had been courted by Finley Peter Dunne, the American political satirist. They married in 1902, settled in New York City and raised four children. Margaret became a friend of Charles Dana Gibson, the celebrated illustrator who drew her portrait in 1903 as one of his famously beautiful "Gibson Girls."

Twenty years after Margaret's death in 1955, Paula Welch, an exercise and sports sciences professor at the University of Florida, cited records that proved Margaret had been an Olympic champion and thus one of the rarest birds in the annals of feminism: a Gold Medal Gibson Girl.

Culver Pictures

Wimbledon Lawn Tennis Museum

The Serena of her day, Charlotte Cooper won five Wimbledon titles as well as the Olympics. (America's Marion Jones, whose namesake would return to the Olympic stage a century later as a track star, tied for third in tennis, though she didn't win a match.) New York City cop **John Flanagan**, an Irish immigrant, won the first of his three Olympic hammer throw titles.

Many sports—jeu de palme, pelota, polo—have come and gone at the Games. In the **tug-of-war**, a combined team from Sweden and Denmark defeats France. In three days, **Alvin Kraenzlein** won not only the 110- and 200-meter hurdles but also the long jump and the since-discontinued 60-meter dash. An **anonymous boy** was recruited by winning Dutch rowers **Roelof Klein** and **François Brandt** to cox their pair-oared shell in another event no longer in the Olympics. The boy may be the youngest Olympic champ ever.

Both golf titles went to Americans in Paris. **Margaret Abbott** finished two strokes ahead of countrywoman Polly Whittier, while **Charles Sands** bested Great Britain's Walter Rutherford by a single shot. Golf left the Games after '04.

1904 *St. Louis*

August 29 to September 3
681 men, **6** women, **12** countries
U.S.A. 238 medals (**80** gold)
All other nations **46** medals (**20** gold)

Because of the daunting distance from Europe to St. Louis, which required a transatlantic voyage followed by a 1,000-mile train ride, plus the notion of an untamed wilderness overrun by savages, European athletes stayed home in droves. As a result, Americans, with 76 percent of all participants, won everything in sight. This was especially propitious for U.S. athletes as gold medals debuted in 1904.

The St. Louis program, again staged as an adjunct to a World's Fair, included an Anthropology Days competition in which costumed members of "the uncivilized tribes"—Pygmies, Moros, Sioux, Ainu, Patagonians—participated in so-called Olympic contests against one another. American white supremacists had a field day with the exhibition, and the official history of the World's Fair pulled no racist punches: "The representatives of the savage and uncivilized tribes proved themselves inferior athletes, greatly overrated."

However, in a lovely moral counterbalance to such thinking, George Poage of the Milwaukee Athletic Club placed third in both the 200- and 400-meter hurdles, becoming the first black man to win a medal in the modern Olympics. Born in Hannibal, Mo., just up the Mississippi River from St. Louis, Poage earned a pre-law degree from the University of Wisconsin in 1903. He was a brilliant orator and scholar as well as a superb quarter-mile runner and hurdler. Poage set national collegiate records in both events and became the first African American to earn membership in the Milwaukee Athletic Club.

After his success in the 1904 Olympics, Poage remained in St. Louis to teach at a high school until 1914 when he returned to Wisconsin and bought a small farm, which he managed till 1920. He moved to Chicago, where he worked in a restaurant for almost four years, then joined the U.S. Postal Service. He remained there for 27 years before retiring. Poage died in 1962.

Courtesy Missouri Historical Society; inset: IOC Olympic Museum Collections

A Pygmy archer competes in an Anthropology Days contest. American Meyer Prinstein, runner-up in Paris four years earlier, wins the "running broad jump," a.k.a. the long jump, with an Olympic record leap of 24' 1".

Yanks on a roll: **Marcus Hurley** won
four cycling events; he later starred
in basketball at Columbia. New Yorker
Fred Winters won silver in a U.S. sweep
of the all-around dumbbell contest. **Ray
Ewry** won golds in two of the three since-
discontinued standing jump events (long jump,
triple jump and high jump). His record of eight golds
won in Paris, St. Louis and London stood for 20 years.

The **swimming events** were held at a lake near the World's Fair building, and featured a starting raft that had an unfortunate tendency to sink. While Americans again took the lion's share of the medals, the freestyle sprints were dominated by the Hungarian Zoltan Halmaj. **George Poage** (circled) made history in the 400-meter hurdles as the first black medal-winner. Bank teller **Harry Hillman** (far left) took the gold.

1908 *London*

July 13 to July 25
1,999 men, **36** women, **23** countries
Great Britain **145** medals (**56** gold)
U.S.A. **47** medals (**23** gold)
Sweden **25** medals (**8** gold)

These Olympics were supposed to have been held in Rome, but the 1906 eruption of Mount Vesuvius forced a change in venue when the Italian government decided to rebuild Naples rather than underwrite a sporting event. London was the stand-in, to American chagrin. Bad feelings between the British hosts and U.S. representatives surfaced early when Old Glory was missing from the forest of national flags flying over Shepherd's Bush Stadium. The animosity grew when the athlete carrying the American flag in the Opening Ceremony, shot-put champ Ralph Rose (left), ignored protocol and refused to dip the Stars and Stripes in tribute to the King of England as he marched past the monarch's stadium seat. The situation got worse when the competition began.

In the marathon, Italian Dorando Pietri wobbled jerkily into the stadium with only the final lap to go. The crowd roared with joy. But because Pietri was suffering from extreme exhaustion, he kept falling, getting up, falling again—four times in all.

Suddenly, American Johnny Hayes entered the stadium, clearly capable of overtaking the Italian. The crowd watched in anxious silence as Pietri fell a fifth time. The Clerk of the Course himself rushed on to the track to help the Italian across the line ahead of Hayes. Later, Pietri was disqualified and Hayes got the gold. Pietri became an instant celebrity and began running exhibitions as a professional.

A different athlete involved in another controversy came to a sadder end.

John Taylor, a recent University of Pennsylvania graduate in veterinary medicine, was favored to win the 400 meters. But after the American runners protested a pro-British ruling in the final by withdrawing from the rerun, he was out of contention. Taylor then ran the third leg of the 4x400 relay and became the first black man to win an Olympic gold medal. Tragically, he died five months later of typhoid at age 26.

Mansell

European Picture Service

Brown Brothers

The saga of **Dorando Pietri** was fraught with drama. Opposite: He's in fine shape on the streets of London, less so in the stadium. With help, he reaches the finish line (above), then receives his ill-gotten gains from Queen Alexandra. Later, justice done, **Johnny Hayes** is on top of the world—and the table.

Irish American **Martin Sheridan** prepares for a standing long jump, in which event he would place third. (He successfully defended his title in the discus and won the Greek-style discus as well.) Oregonian **Forrest Smithson** *was* devout and *did* win the 110-meter hurdles, but this famous photo of him with his Bible was posed. World-record holder **Harold Wilson** of Great Britain was leading the 1,500 meters until **Mel Sheppard** of the U.S. sprints past him 15 yards from the finish to win the first of his four golds.

1912 *Stockholm*

July 6 to July 15
2,490 men, **57** women, **28** countries
Sweden **65** medals (**24** gold)
U.S.A. **61** medals (**23** gold)

The grandest hero of the Stockholm Games was neither Scandinavian nor European but a brilliant, full-blooded Native American named Jim Thorpe, who won both the decathlon and the pentathlon. When Sweden's King Gustav V gave Thorpe his prizes he declared, "You, sir, are the greatest athlete in the world." Thorpe may or may not have replied, "Thanks, King," as legend has it, yet Gustav was correct. Thorpe was an All-America halfback while playing football in 1911 and 1912 for the tiny Pennsylvania reservation college, Carlisle. He earned varsity letters in 11 different sports. What's more, in 1912 he won the intercollegiate ballroom dancing championship.

In Stockholm, the 24-year-old Thorpe broke the world record for the decathlon by 998 points and finished first in four of the five events in the pentathlon. Back home, he was overwhelmed by a ticker-tape parade down Broadway in New York City: "I heard people yelling my name—and I couldn't realize how one fellow could have so many friends."

In 1913, Thorpe was stripped of his medals after a newspaper reported he had been paid—perhaps as little as $2 a game—while playing semipro baseball a few years earlier. The gold medals then went to the two men who had finished second, Swede Hugo Wieslander in the decathlon and Norwegian Ferdinand Bie in the pentathlon. Neither relished his reward. Bie told friends, "I do not consider it the first prize." Wieslander said, "Thorpe was the best man. I wasn't. He should have the medal."

In 1950 an Associated Press sportswriters' poll named Thorpe the greatest athlete of the first half of the 20th century. In the mid-'60s, Wieslander, now an old man, tried to find Thorpe and return the medal. His quest failed. "No one knew where he was," Wieslander told friends. "So I had to keep the medal." Wieslander couldn't locate his former adversary because Thorpe had already died—penniless in a trailer in Lomita, Calif., in 1953. Both medals were returned to his family in January 1983.

The decathlon and pentathlon were grueling tests, with jumping, throwing and running events—ranging from a 100-meter dash to the decathlon's climactic 1,500-meter run—staged in quick succession. **Jim Thorpe** made them look easy, impressing the king as much as the fans in the stands.

The regal bearing of Hawaii's **Duke Paoa Kahinu Makoe Hulikohoa Kahanamoku**—you can call him Duke— enthralled swim fans in 1912, and would for years to come. He won the 100-meter freestyle; did so again in 1920 on his 30th birthday; and placed second in the 1924 Games in Paris. His female equivalent in Stockholm was Australian **Fanny Durack**, who would one day hold every women's world record from 100 yards to one mile, and who won the Olympic 100 meters by a country mile, leading start to finish. Finishing second to Durack was another Australian, Mina Wylie, and trailing the Aussies were the **British swimmers** (top right), who had the largest contingent in the first women's Olympic swim race.

The chief beneficiary of a Greco-Roman wrestling bout between **Martin Klein** of Russia (right) and **Alfred Asikainen** of Finland was Claes Johanson of Sweden. In this semifinal, the men battled for *11 hours* before Klein pinned Asikainen. The winner was too spent to compete in the final against the Swede.

At 4' 7" and 65 lb, **Aileen Riggin** was Antwerp's smallest competitor. But the native of Newport, R.I., took the gold for springboard diving, and at 14 was the youngest official champion to date. Opposite: The great **Paavo Nurmi** began his ascent to immortality at the 1920 Games.

1920 *Antwerp*

August 14 to August 29
2,543 men, **64** women, **29** countries
U.S.A. **96** medals (**41** gold)
Sweden **63** medals (**19** gold)
Great Britain **43** medals (**15** gold)
Belgium **35** medals (**14** gold)

Mourning over World War I went on long after the Armistice was signed in November 1918. When the Antwerp Games began 20 months later, people still didn't feel much like celebrating. At one point, Belgium's King Albert summed up the scene: "All this is quite nice, but it certainly lacks people."

Antwerp marked the debut of the premier distance runner in Olympic history—the Flying Finn, Paavo Nurmi. He won gold medals in the 10,000 meters and two cross-country races, then continued to dominate his events in 1924 and '28, taking nine golds and three silvers in all. No one else has ever come close to his superhuman performance of setting world records at every distance he tried—22 records in all, from 1,500 to 20,000 meters.

Nurmi had grown up poor in Turku, a rural settlement where he sometimes raced a mail train as it passed through the forest. Despite competing as an amateur, Nurmi took many under-the-table payments; it was said he possessed "the lowest heartbeat and highest asking price of any athlete in the world." He escaped censure until 1932 when he was disqualified for the L.A. Olympic marathon.

In later life, he became a recluse, known for his real estate holdings and his stinginess. At one point in the late 1960s, he granted reporters an audience.

"Did you ever think of yourself as running for your homeland?" he was asked.

"I ran for myself, never for Finland," he said.

"Not even in the Olympics?"

"Above all, not then. At the Olympics, Paavo Nurmi mattered more than ever."

Was he always so self-absorbed? Word got out in the early '70s that Nurmi was renting a Helsinki apartment for half price to the aged and sick Finnish runner Ville Ritola, the only man to defeat him in the Olympics. The two hadn't liked each other, but apparently Nurmi had a change of heart in his old age. He died soon after, in 1973, at the age of 76.

Charley Paddock was born in Texas, and was a sickly child. By his mid-teens, however, he had developed into a robust, formidable runner. Here, as he breaks the tape in the 100 meters, he demonstrates his renowned "flying finish," in which he wowed crowds by leaping when he was a full four yards from the finish line.

1924 *Paris*

July 5 to July 27
2,956 men, **136** women, **44** countries
U.S.A. 99 medals (**45** gold)
France 38 medals (**13** gold)
Finland 37 medals (**14** gold)

Baron de Coubertin asked, as a favor, that Paris host the 1924 Games because he had decided to retire as IOC president. Despite a few bad episodes (some fanatical French fans booed during other nations' anthems, and the entire British team threatened to walk out owing to the overwhelming success of America's "professionals"), these Games turned out to be the best so far. Enthusiastic crowds ranged up to 64,000 a day. When it was over, de Coubertin said happily, "My work is done."

Two American medal winners in Paris are worthy of note. Benjamin Spock, 21, later the well-known baby doctor, rowed for Yale's triumphant eight-oar crew. William DeHart Hubbard, 20, a Cincinnati-born student at the University of Michigan, took the long jump to become the first black man in history to win an individual gold medal.

Harold Abrahams, an ebullient British sprinter who trained on cigars and ale, was the surprise winner of the 100-meter dash, an event commemorated in the 1981 film *Chariots of Fire*. Abrahams went on to become a renowned barrister in London as well as a commentator and writer. Late in his life he was asked what had motivated him to perform at such a peak. "There was a certain amount of anti-Semitism about," he said. "Certainly, I didn't run in the Olympics to win for all of the Jews. I ran for myself. But I felt I had become something of an outsider, you know. That may have helped."

A man's religion was the big part of the story for the other *Chariots* protagonist. Eric Liddell, a devout Christian, withdrew from the 100 meters because he would not run heats scheduled for Sunday. But the Scotsman came through smashingly in the 400.

For all the drama, there was still far less Sturm und Drang than there is in the movie. "When we won, there was hardly any fuss," said Abrahams. "There was no victory ceremony that I recall. I just remember some handclapping when I went into dinner with the team that night."

Brown Brothers

On the day he ran the race of his life, **Harold Abrahams**, above, took to heart the words of his coach: "Only think of two things—the report of the pistol and the tape. When you hear the one, just run like hell till you break the other." **Eric Liddell** had a catch-phrase that served him well: "I do not like to be beaten." In Paris, no one could top him in the 400 meters. Liddell died in a Japanese internment camp during WWI.

At left, a view of the first **Olympic Village**, humble by today's standards. Above, **Paavo Nurmi** clears the last wall before winning the 10,000-meter cross-country. It would be the last Olympic cross-country race. Nurmi was, of course, fine. The others, however, were utterly undone by the brutal event.

William DeHart Hubbard leaps to a gold medal in the long jump. (The silver medalist, Edward Gourdin, would later become the first African American member of the Massachusetts Superior Court.) Incidentally, it should be noted that in the rules governing the long jump, it is stated that no somersaults are allowed. Clearly this is not an event for those with a flair for the absurd.

1928 *Amsterdam*

July 28 to August 12
2,724 men, **290** women, **46** countries
U.S.A. **56** medals (**22** gold)
Germany **31** medals (**10** gold)
Holland **19** medals (**6** gold)

Though still a woefully small Olympic minority, women competed in larger numbers in Amsterdam than ever before. In earlier Games, they had golfed, swum, dived or played tennis, but in 1928 they could compete in track and field, always the core sport. The first Olympic women's field event was the discus throw, won by Poland's Halina Konopacka. The first track event was the 100-meter dash, won by American Betty Robinson. The 16-year-old high-school student from Illinois had been discovered as a sprinter by a teacher, who saw her running to catch a school bus.

The leading man in Amsterdam was the tall, handsome American swimmer Johnny Weissmuller, who added two golds to his three from Paris. The son of a coal miner, Weissmuller became the foremost swimmer of his day, and used his renown to earn millions as an actor playing Tarzan. "I was in training for the 1932 Olympics," he once recalled, "when I was offered a five-year, $500-a-week contract with BVD swimming suits. I'd go around swimming shows and tell people, 'You swim faster in our suits.' One day in L.A., they asked me to do a screen test for Tarzan. I ran around in a loincloth and climbed a tree and picked up this girl and carried her around. There were 150 Tarzans trying out, and I went back to selling BVD suits. Then I got a wire: COME BACK. YOU'RE TARZAN.

"When I got to Hollywood, the producer told me my name was too long to fit on a marquee. The director said, 'Don't you know who this is? This is the greatest swimmer in the history of the world.' So the producer said, 'O.K., keep your name. We'll write some swimming into the picture.'"

Weissmuller was the first of four Olympic medalists—Buster Crabbe, Herman Brix and Glenn Morris were the others—to play Tarzan, and he did it 11 times in 16 years. He went from rich to poor several times in his life. When he died in Acapulco in 1984, he was broke and living with his fifth wife.

Brown Brothers

Bettmann/Corbis

Teenager **Betty Robinson** was naturally gifted with speed; she had never run a race before 1928, but came to the Olympics—her fourth track meet—as world-record holder at 100 meters. In 1931 she was nearly killed in a small plane crash, but after recovering from severe injuries she returned to the track and, in 1936, won a second gold in the 4x100-meter relay. **Johnny Weissmuller,** even as an athlete, has his matinee-idol smile down pat.

Germany's **Lina Radke** beats Japan's **Kinue Hitomi** in the 800 meters, setting a world record that will last for 16 years. Though the race was thrilling, the women's exhausted appearance at the finish, where some competitors collapsed, prompted officials to banish the event. (It would return to the Games in 1960.) In the men's 10,000, archrival Finns **Ville Ritola** (left), the defending champion, and **Paavo Nurmi** run neck and neck for 24 laps before Nurmi surges to the line, claiming his ninth and final gold.

As synchronized swimming and rhythmic gymnastics would later confirm, the Olympics are a setting not only for drama and excitement but also fun. In Amsterdam, **judges at the diving events** use bathing chairs to shield themselves from their colleagues' undue influence. The **Dutch royal family** is serenity itself as cross-country competitors labor past the tennis courts. And, in the first year female gymnasts competed in the Olympics, the **French team** climbs the ropes. The Dutch women won the team combined event. Four of the 10 were Jewish; three of them would die in Nazi gas chambers.

1932 *Los Angeles*

July 30 to August 14
1,281 men, **127** women, **37** countries
U.S.A. **104** medals (**41** gold)
Italy **36** medals (**12** gold)
France **19** medals (**10** gold)

Thanks to the worldwide Depression and the long trip required to get from almost anywhere else to the U.S. Pacific coast, the Los Angeles Games drew the smallest field of competitors since the 1904 Olympics, also staged in America. Just six months before the Games were to begin, not a single nation had agreed to attend.

The heroine of these Olympics was a brash Texan who ultimately became the tomboy belle of Los Angeles. When Mildred "Babe" Didrikson was asked how she'd do in the Games, she bragged, "I came out to beat everybody in sight, and that's just what I'm going to do. I can do anything." And she could. She won two golds—in the 80-meter hurdles and in the javelin throw—plus a silver in the high jump.

She rode her Olympic fame for a time after the Games, performing in a vaudeville act in which she played the harmonica and jogged on a treadmill while singing "I'm Fit As a Fiddle and Ready for Love." She also pitched for the touring House of David baseball team and traveled with an exhibition basketball team called Babe Didrikson's All-Americans.

In the mid-1930s she began playing serious golf, and her dear friend and admirer, sportswriter Grantland Rice, penned one of his trademark bits of doggerel for her: "From the high jump of Olympic fame, the hurdles and the rest/The javelin that flashed its fame on by the record test/The Texas Babe now shifts the scene where slashing drives are far/Where spoon shots find the distant green to break the back of par."

Babe went on breaking the back of par until she became certifiably the finest woman golfer of her day. She died in 1956 at the tragically young age of 45 after a long, pain-wracked siege of cancer. To Rice she was the best athlete, male or female, of all time: "the most flawless section of muscle harmony, of complete mental and physical coordination the world of sport has ever seen."

Bettmann/Corbis

Clockwise from above: Babe Didrikson tied for first in the high jump, sharing a new world record with fellow American Jean Shiley, but was reduced to second because of her head-first jumping technique; she set a world record again in winning the hurdles; and she threw the javelin more than 143 feet.

Getty Images

AP Wide World

Two outsize celebrities were American swimmers **Eleanor Holm** and **Buster Crabbe**, both of whom starred in La La Land, then went on to greater fame in other affairs. Brooklynite Holm was 18 when she won the 100-meter backstroke in 1932; four years later she was kicked off the Olympic team for drinking during the sail to Europe. (She then spent time during the Olympic fortnight socializing with Nazis: "Göring was fun.") Holm, a sometime actress (she was Jane in *Tarzan's Revenge*), died earlier this year. As for the Californian Crabbe, after he won the 400-meter freestyle in L.A., Paramount tabbed him as its answer to MGM's Johnny Weissmuller. Crabbe played Tarzan, Flash Gordon, Billy the Kid and other legends in dozens of films. He died in 1983.

In Los Angeles, the Games of ancient Greece got an early taste of the glamorous, glittering aspect that would fully attend them in the television era. Not all swimsuits were on the swimmers, and luminaries in the stands included such as **Fay Wray**, **Amelia Earhart** and **Douglas Fairbanks**. Two friends, **Ralph Metcalfe** and **Eddie Tolan**, became stars of a different sort at the Coliseum with a sensational duel in the 100 meters. Tolan nipped Metcalfe by two inches, and both finished in 10.3 seconds.

1936 *Berlin*

August 1 to August 16
3,738 men, **328** women, **49** countries
Germany **89** medals (**33** gold)
U.S.A. **56** medals (**24** gold)
German government spent a mind-boggling
$30 million to create an Aryan showcase.

In 1931 the IOC had selected Berlin as host for the 1936 Olympics. When Adolf Hitler took control of the German government in early '33, he decided to turn the Games into a propaganda tool: He would use them to display his notion of Nazi racial and technological superiority while creating the impression that his intentions were peaceful. The Nazis built a 41-country radio network and introduced Telex facilities to transmit press reports and zeppelin service to courier newsreels. Unknown to the world, the Olympic Village, which housed 3,700 male athletes during the Games, was designed for quick post-Olympic conversion to military use.

Hitler's plan to use the Olympics to enhance the world image of his Third Reich was successful—especially when Germany left all other nations far behind in the medal count. However, his racist haranguing about Aryan white supremacy was muted by the noble American black man who was the superstar of these Nazi Games.

Born the son of an illiterate Alabama sharecropper, James C. "Jesse" Owens recalled an arduous childhood: "We picked cotton all day long. When I was seven, I was picking 100 pounds a day." The family moved to Cleveland, and Jesse became a star on the Ohio State track team. He once accomplished the astounding feat of breaking five world records and tying a sixth in a single afternoon. His four gold medals in Berlin—the 100-meter and 200-meter dashes, the 4x100 relay and the long jump—made him a hero even in Germany.

When Owens returned home, he was honored with ticker-tape parades, and he later prospered as an inspirational speaker. "Until the '30s, the Negro had no image to point to," he once said. "Then there were two—Joe Louis and myself. We were riding the wave of newfound pride that the Negro had then. I hope we've never let them down." A heavy smoker, he died in 1980 at age 66 of lung cancer.

Bettmann/Corbis

Bettmann/Corbis; inset: Lothar Rübelt/IOC Olympic Museum Collections

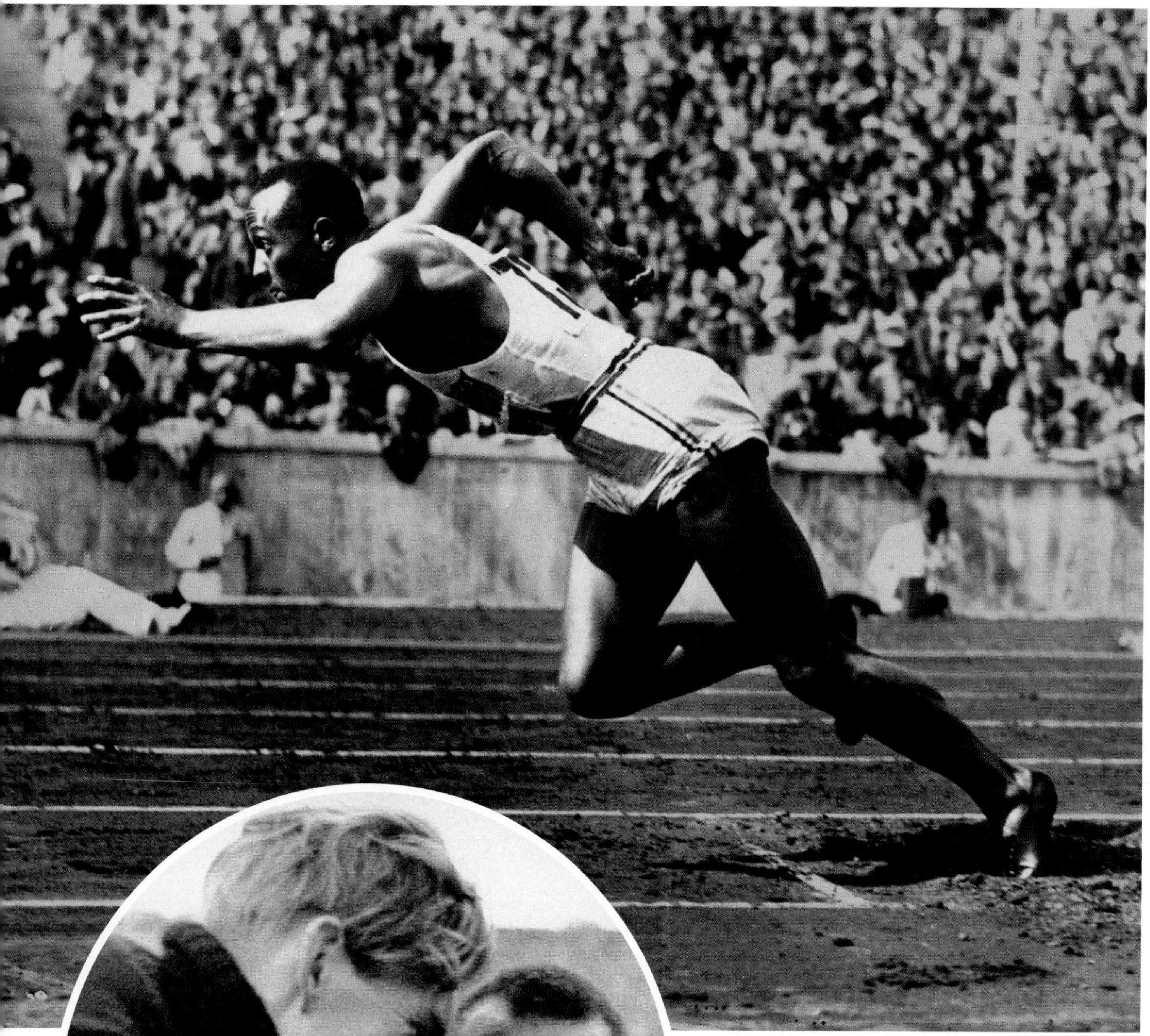

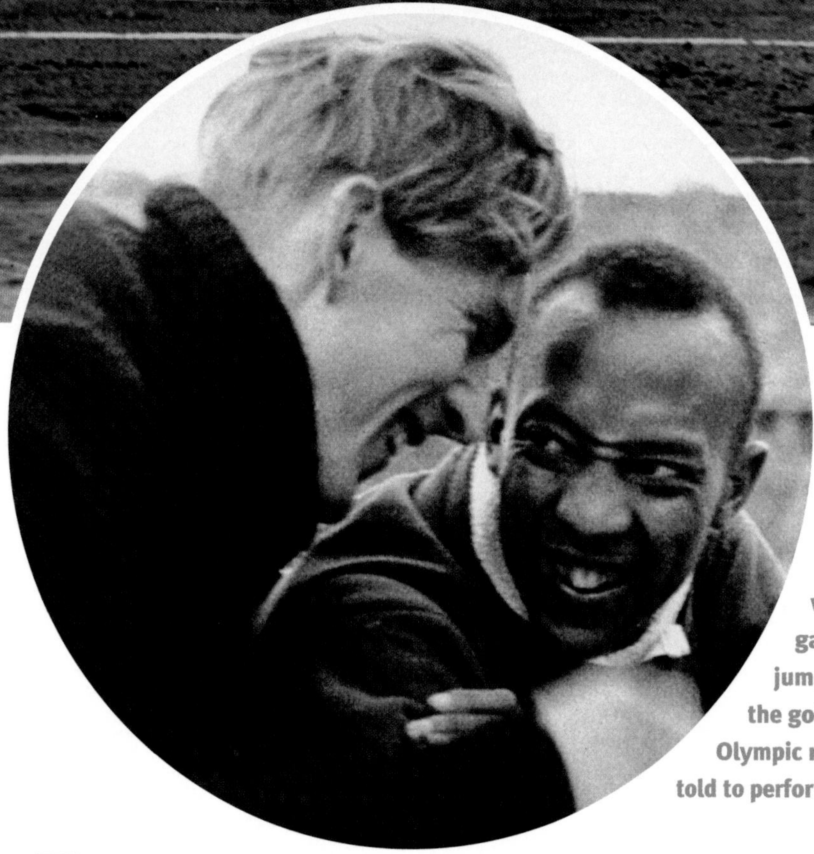

Never was an athletic performance so freighted with significance as that of **Jesse Owens** in the Berlin arena. Though Hitler did not shake the black man's hand, Owens was treated well by most German athletes, particularly his toughest long-jump rival. **Luz Long**, seen here sharing a joke and also the podium with Owens, not only befriended the American but also gave him a technical tip about his takeoff during the long-jump competition. The advice ultimately helped Owens win the gold at Long's expense. Above: Owens speeds toward his Olympic record 26' 5 ½" jump. Right: German athletes were told to perform the Nazi salute, no matter whose anthem was playing.

AP Wide World

American women, too, competed admirably at the Olympics. **Helen Stephens** of Fulton, Mo., blows away the field in the 100 meters, winning in a world-record time, 11.5 seconds. Scouting the pool is Los Angeles native **Marjorie Gestring**, who will become the youngest person in Summer Olympic history to win an individual gold medal by taking the springboard diving event at age 13 years, nine months. The German gold-medal hammer thrower **Karl Hein** is captured in action by Adolf Hitler's propagandist photographer and filmmaker Leni Riefenstahl, who during the Games shoots *Olympia*.

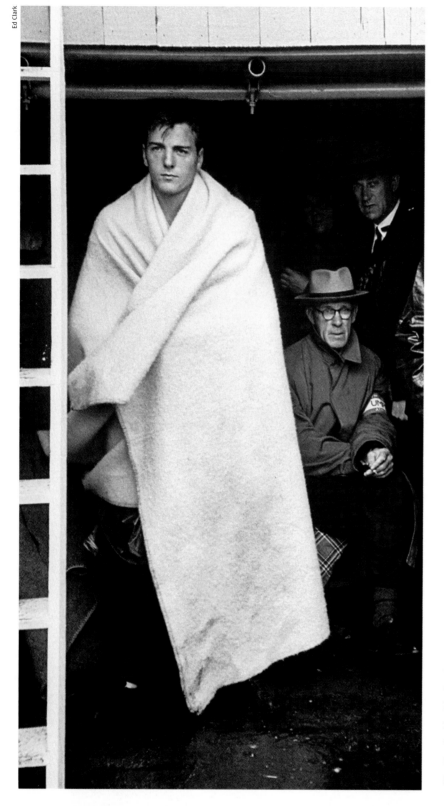

A weary **Bob Mathias** awaits the pole vault. His fame would become phenomenal. He starred in football at Stanford. In 1954 he played the lead in the movie *The Bob Mathias Story*. He served from 1967 to '74 as a four-term U.S. Congressman from California. And he graced the front of a box of Wheaties. Opposite: Despite tripping over the fifth barrier and stumbling to the tape, **Fanny Blankers-Koen** won the 80-meter hurdles.

1948 *London*

July 29 to August 14
3,714 men, **385** women, **59** countries
Axis nations not invited
U.S.A. **84** medals (**38** gold)
Great Britain **23** medals (**3** gold)

Although the Second World War had been over for almost three years, food was still rationed and rubble-filled ruins were still common in bomb-devastated London. Nevertheless the city, which had hosted in 1908 and had been slated to do so again in 1944, was chosen to welcome the athletes back to the Olympic arena after a dozen-year absence. London did the best it could, but with money short, an RAF barracks served as the Olympic Village. Many teams had to bring their own food.

The most notable star of the Games was Holland's Francina Elsje "Fanny" Blankers-Koen. The 30-year-old mother of two won four gold medals, in the 100- and 200-meter dashes, the 80-meter hurdles and the 4x100 relay. She surely would have had a fifth gold if the schedule had let her enter the long jump, in which she held the world record.

Though the sports-page headline writers dubbed her the Flying Housewife, many women in the Netherlands had, before the Games, criticized Blankers-Koen as a derelict wife and mother, because her training interfered with her "proper" duties as a homemaker. She retorted that she took time to train only twice a week "between washing dishes and darning socks."

The criticism ceased after her historic performance in London. The people of Amsterdam paraded her around in a horse-drawn carriage, named a rose and a candy bar after her and erected a statue in her honor. In 1999, Blankers-Koen was voted by the International Association of Athletics Federations the "best female athlete of the 20th century." She died this past January in Holland at age 85.

As a young child, Bob Mathias suffered from anemia, but a complex regimen permitted him to become a tremendous athlete by the time he was a teenager. At 17 he became the youngest person to win a men's athletic event, and it was one of the most demanding: the decathlon. Mathias became one of America's immortal sports heroes.

Heavyweight champion Greco-Roman wrestler **Ahmet Kirecci** is lifted up by jubilant Turkish countrymen. The short-armed American bantamweight **Joseph DePietro** could hardly get the barbell over his head but still took the gold. **Bob Mathias** had never attempted the decathlon until just four months before the Olympics—he used a manual to learn the pole vault and javelin—but he went on to win the gold medal and then repeated in the '52 Games.

Ed Clark

Alpha/Empics (2)

An array of top divers gather at poolside: **Bruce Harlan** (U.S.), **Charles Johnson** (U.K.), **Sammy Lee**, **Vicki Draves**, **Juno Stover** (all U.S.) and **Peter Heatly** (U.K.). Opposite: **Draves**, who hailed from San Francisco, became the first Asian American (she had a Filipino father and an English mother) competitor to medal when she went gold in both springboard and platform. In the exciting conclusion to the 100-meter dash, Cleveland's **Harrison Dillard** edges out teammate **Barney Ewell.** This picture marks the first time that a photo-finish camera was used at the Olympic Games.

1952 *Helsinki*

July 19 to August 3
4,407 men, **518** women, **69** countries
U.S.A. **76** medals (**40** gold)
U.S.S.R. **71** medals (**22** gold)
Finland **22** medals (**6** gold)

This was the first Olympics for the U.S.S.R., and no one knew what to expect. "For all we knew, the Russians had a guy who could throw the shot 80 feet and another who could high jump nine feet," said America's shot-put champion, Parry O'Brien.

The real hero in Helsinki was neither Russian nor American. Czechoslovakia's Emil Zatopek performed an unprecedented feat by winning gold in the 5,000- and 10,000-meter runs plus the marathon. This was all the more amazing because it was the first marathon he had ever run in competition, and he won it by more than two minutes.

Zatopek was jokingly known as Emil the Terrible because he always grimaced, gasped, groaned and writhed during races as if he had a scorpion in each shoe and a python wrapped around his chest. Asked about this weird behavior, Zatopek replied lightly, "I was not talented enough to run and smile at the same time." But he was talented enough to win four golds and a silver in the Games of '48 and '52, and to set 18 world records in his career.

His beloved wife, Dana, was also a star, winning gold in the javelin in '52, finishing fourth in '56 and taking silver in '60, 18 days short of her 38th birthday. This achievement made her the oldest woman in Olympic history to win a track and field medal.

As for Emil, win or lose, he adored the Games: "The Olympics are the one true time. At the Olympics you can say, 'These men are the best.'" His triumphs against the best won him a promotion to colonel in the Czech Army. But in 1968, during the Prague Spring rebellion that was ultimately crushed by Soviet tanks, he signed the 2,000-Word Manifesto calling for his country's freedom. He was dismissed from the army, expelled from the Party and was assigned such manual-labor jobs as ditchdigger, well-tester and garbage collector. He survived it all, and when democracy replaced communism, he was a national hero again—which is what he was when he died, at age 78, in 2000.

Pressfoto

The Opening Ceremony crowd leaps to its feet as none other than Paavo Nurmi, 55 years old and a certified national treasure, runs into the stadium with the Olympic flame. Nurmi will hand the torch to another Finnish legend, Hannes Kolehmainen, 62, patriarch of the great Finn distance runners. It falls to Kolehmainen, who won three gold medals in 1912 as well as the 1920 marathon, to light the cauldron.

Mark Kauffman (2)

Life was a romance beyond compare for **the Zatopeks** in Helsinki—and long thereafter. They had met in 1948 at a competition in Czechoslovakia where both set national records. Emil proposed during the London Olympics, meanwhile winning the 10,000 meters and finishing second in the 5,000 (Dana placed seventh in the javelin). After Emil won the 5,000 in 1952, Dana said to him, "Please give me your medal for good luck." He dutifully did so, and she had it with her that afternoon when she set a new Olympic javelin record of 165' 7'' on her first attempt (above). Once Emil had his two track golds, he joked that he would have to enter the marathon to further trump his wife. Then he did so, and won that, too (opposite). The Zatopeks grew old together in Prague, where they walked and cycled in Stromovka Park.

Like the champion high jumper Ray Ewry of the Olympics'
early years, **Buddy Davis** was a survivor of childhood polio; he
couldn't walk for three years after being stricken at age eight.
In 1952 he set a new Olympic record, and in '53 broke a 12-year-
old world mark by clearing 6' 11 ⅝''. Davis went on to a pro
basketball career. French swimmer **Jean Boiteux and his père**

are happily drenched after the former won the 400-meter
freestyle, and the latter leaped into the pool to congratulate
him. Californian **Pat McCormick** won two golds in Helsinki by
taking the springboard and platform diving events. America's
finest-ever female diver was doubly golden again four years
later, winning in Melbourne eight months after giving birth.

November 22 to December 8
2,958 men, **384** women, **67** countries
U.S.S.R. **98** medals (**37** gold)
U.S.A. **74** medals (**32** gold)
Australia **35** medals (**13** gold)

In 1956 political flash fires burned around the world, most notably the Suez Crisis and the rebellion of Hungarian freedom fighters against Soviet domination. Even so, the atmosphere in Melbourne was conspicuously unwarlike—most of the time. Much attention was paid to a bloody water-polo match in which the Hungarian team walloped the Soviets 4–0 for the gold medal before the game was called due to violence. But this was an exception.

Although Soviet gymnast Larysa Latynina won four golds, the athletes who shone brightest in the southern sun were two Aussie golden girls, swimmer Dawn Fraser (two golds and a silver) and sprinter Betty Cuthbert (three golds). Another child of Oz, swimmer Murray Rose, became the first man since Johnny Weissmuller to win a pair of individual freestyle events.

The biggest spectacle of the '56 Games came at the Closing Ceremony, when athletes spilled together in a polyglot mix of humanity—dancing, singing, laughing and weeping as they created a new Olympic form for celebrating people over politics.

Another Olympic symbol first seen in Australia was Al Oerter. His saga would go on until he won his fourth straight gold in the discus 12 years later. Never was he the favorite, and never did he hold the world record, yet he set an Olympic mark with every victory. In Mexico City he won for the last time with a powerful throw of 212' 6"—more than five feet farther than he had ever flung a discus before.

Oerter retired before the '72 Games, then couldn't resist trying for a comeback eight years later. Though he didn't make the team (which, in any event, was derailed by boycott), his effort illustrated his old-fashioned amateur attitude toward discus-throwing. "I've always viewed it as a recreation," he said. "You work four years for a medal, and throw it in a drawer."

John Zimmerman/Sports Illustrated

Bettmann/Corbis (2)

Homebred heroes: Above, the sensational **Dawn Fraser**, the youngest of eight children, would strike gold again in Rome; dubbed the Seaweed Streak because of his vegetarian diet, **Murray Rose** (left) had a lot of swimmers looking at their own menus; **Betty Cuthbert** won the 100- and 200-meter sprints, and also received a gold for anchoring the victorious Australian 4x100 relay team (right).

A mere three weeks after the U.S.S.R. sent troops into Hungary to squelch an uprising, the water-polo teams from these two nations met in Melbourne. In a sport already known for its rough-and-tumble play, a nasty fight ended the contest. Above, Hungary's **Ervin Zador**. At left, West Babylon, N.Y.'s **Al Oerter** prepares to unfurl yet another throw of the discus in a career of truly remarkable breadth. The darling of the gymnastics competition was 21-year-old **Larysa Latynina** of the Ukraine. She took home four gold medals, including the all-around, right, and also snared a silver and a bronze.

John Dominis

Bettmann/Corbis

Tom Hutchins

The field of athletics is a testing ground, and sometimes winning requires a very great sacrifice. This is always so in the Olympics. Above, after finishing first in the marathon, Algerian-born Frenchman **Alain Mimoun** props his feet up on the No. 1 stand and nurses a beverage. At left, **Caldwell Esselstyn** sheds a tear of relief as his crewmates congratulate him after their victory in the eight-oared shell with coxswain. The team from Yale had won the right to represent the United States. Opposite, **Lou Jones** and **Charley Jenkins** hold each other up after finishing one of track's most punishing races, the 400 meters. Jenkins was the winner, while his teammate Jones came in fifth.

1960 *Rome*

August 25 to September 11
4,738 men, **610** women, **83** countries
U.S.S.R. **103** medals (**43** gold)
U.S.A. **81** medals (**34** gold)
Italy **36** medals (**13** gold)
First international TV coverage; CBS bought
U.S. rights for **$50,000**.

Played out before the classic architecture of ancient Rome, these Games were as beautiful—and as full of good cheer, good works and goodwill—as any in decades. The Roman Olympic Organizing Committee struck a deal with the Association of Roman Thieves to prevent street crimes during the Games, and local authorities received fewer complaints about pickpockets, purse snatchers, car thieves and muggers than in many years.

Two young African Americans from the South starred in Rome. Sprinter Wilma Rudolph, 20, won three golds—in the 100 meters, 200 meters and 4x100 relay. She became the toast of the European press, nicknamed La Perle Noire by the French, Wilma-on-the-Wing by the British and La Gazzella Nera by the Italians. Cassius Clay, 18, later Muhammad Ali, won boxing gold in the light-heavyweight division.

Rome's marathon, staged at night over ancient streets lit with torches, was won by Abebe Bikila, 28, a private in the Ethiopian Imperial Bodyguard who ran barefoot over the cobblestones of the Appian Way, taking the first of his two Olympic titles.

Long a hero in his country, Bikila became almost a holy man after he was permanently paralyzed from the waist down following an auto accident in March 1969. Children, Ethiopian soldiers and world-class runners made pilgrimages to his modest cottage on the outskirts of Addis Ababa where he sat in his wheelchair, dispensing wisdom and advice. Once, someone asked him if he was bitter about the fate that transformed him from Olympic runner to paraplegic, and he replied, "I was overjoyed when I won the marathon twice. But I accepted those victories as I accept this tragedy. I have no choice. I have to accept both circumstances as facts of life, and live happily." In 1973 this noble man died of a brain hemorrhage. He was 41.

Abebe Bikila's face was set in a beatific mask for most of the 26 miles of the marathon. Then he crossed the finish line at the Arch of Constantine and burst into a radiant smile. He shattered Emil Zatopek's Olympic record by almost eight minutes, and was the first black African to win a marathon. Four years later, in Tokyo, Bikila would win again.

John Zimmerman/Sports Illustrated

The U.S. Olympic boxing team is anchored by a smiling teenager known at the time as **Cassius Clay** (above, far right). His charm and charisma were already in evidence, and he captivated the fans as he captured the gold. Below, the women of the U.S. track team, including star **Wilma Rudolph** (below, left), delight in seeing the fountains of Rome. Right: Back at work on the track, Rudolph, who had already beaten polio, double pneumonia and scarlet fever as a child in Tennessee, beats **Dorothy Hyman** (center) of Great Britain and **Giuseppina Leone** of Italy in the 100 meters. She also won the gold over 200 meters.

Mark Kauffman

In the lane closest to the camera, West Germany's **Armin Hary**, renowned for his "blitz start," is off and running toward a gold medal in the men's 100 meters. A leg injury suffered in a car crash after the Games would end Hary's career. Left: Ukranian **Vira Krepkina**, competing for the U.S.S.R., is elated after popping an Olympic-record 20' 10 ¾" long jump. She was already a coholder of the world record in the 100-meter dash.

One of the most affecting stories of this or any Olympics was that of **Yang Chuan-kwang** and **Rafer Johnson**, rivals—and friends. C.K. Yang, as he was known, was a native of Taiwan who was studying at U.C.L.A., where Johnson was also a collegiate track star. They battled mightily in the decathlon over two long days, and then, before the final event, the 1,500 meters, each man approached his coach—the same man, U.C.L.A.'s legendary **Ducky Drake**. Drake told Yang to pull away, Johnson to stay close. Johnson was able to, barely: He finished only six yards behind, and secured the gold.

1964 *Tokyo*

October 10 to October 24
4,457 men, **683** women, **93** countries
U.S.A. **90** medals (**36** gold)
U.S.S.R. **86** medals (**30** gold)
Japan **29** medals (**16** gold)

The Japanese spent almost $2 billion, more than any previous host. For this outlay they got one of the best Olympics ever—and much more. The Games transformed Japan's reputation and economic position. As Tokyo Mayor Dr. Ryotaro Azuma put it: "We were still struggling under a defeated-enemy-nation syndrome in the eyes of most of the world. Without the magic of the Olympic name we might never have gotten the investment we needed to rise as a world trade power."

American Don Schollander became the first swimmer to win four gold medals in a single Games—in the 100- and 400-meter freestyle races, and the 400- and 800-meter free relays—but the biggest headlines went to Australia's Dawn Fraser.

In Tokyo, Fraser, a ripe old 27, won her third straight gold medal in the 100-meter freestyle, becoming the only swimmer ever to win the same event in three consecutive Games. This wasn't the reason she became a hot story, however. Fraser celebrated her victory with a few beers, then led a midnight raid to swipe a flag from the Imperial Palace. She was arrested, but charges were dropped. In fact, the Tokyo police gave her the flag as a gift. Aussie swimming authorities were less forgiving, banning her from competition for 10 years. Fraser explained that she had been under immense emotional pressure: "In March 1964, I was in a bad car accident, and my mother was killed. I had been driving the car, and now my mother was dead . . . I was nearing a mental breakdown. I wanted nothing but to win the gold medal for my mother." When the swimming union was unyielding, Fraser successfully sued for defamation: "They said I swam in the emperor's moat—in the nude. None of the things they said were true."

Fraser remained a heroine to Australian sports fans, and in 1990 was elected to the New South Wales parliament. During Sydney's Olympic fortnight in 2000, "Our Dawn" was feted dawn to dusk.

George Silk

The fog rolls in at Lake Sagami during the medal ceremony in the women's 500-meter kayak pairs event. West Germans Roswitha Esser and Annemarie Zimmermann are golden. Second place goes to 15-year-old Francine Fox and 35-year-old Gloriane Perrier of the U.S. The bronze medalists are Hilde Lauer and Cornelia Sideri of Romania.

The Australian veteran **Dawn Fraser** is flanked by American young 'uns **Sharon Stouder** (left) and **Kathleen Ellis** after they place 1-2-3 in the 100. Fraser would soon be off on the escapade that led to her 10-year ban. While that suspension was finally reduced to four years, she never swam in a world-class race again. Swim star **Don Schollander**, giving the thumbs-up after one of his four Tokyo wins, would return to the Olympic pool in the 1968 Games, adding a fifth gold in a relay and a silver in the 200-meter freestyle. The native of North Carolina, who grew up in Oregon and trained in California, is welcomed back to the States by his parents.

A tradition that has obtained since the birth of the modern Olympics is that the United States does well in the sprints. The Georgian **Wyomia Tyus** (left, breaking the tape) won the 100 meters in Tokyo and again in 1968 in Mexico City, where she lowered the world record to 11.08 seconds. **Edith McGuire** (runner-up in the 100 and, opposite, winning the 200) was Tyus's teammate at Tennessee State. **Bob Hayes**, "the world's fastest human," wins the 100 by seven feet. Later, he was a star pass receiver for the Dallas Cowboys. NFL coaches invented zone defenses to deal with his blinding speed.

There had been discussions of an African American boycott of the Games, but when that didn't happen, 200-meter gold medalist Tommie Smith and his San Jose State teammate John Carlos mounted the podium shoeless, with gloved fists and wearing buttons in support of the Olympic Project for Human Rights. Runner-up Peter Norman of Australia wore an OPHR button too.

1968 *Mexico City*

October 12 to October 27
4,750 men, **781** women, **112** countries
U.S.A. **107** medals (**45** gold)
U.S.S.R. **91** medals (**29** gold)
Mexico **9** medals (**3** gold)

Mexico City was in political turmoil even before the Olympics began, as army forces killed dozens of rioting students in the Plaza of Three Cultures on October 2. The Games themselves seethed with political volatility. To protest U.S. racial policies, American sprinters Tommie Smith and John Carlos raised black-gloved fists on the victory stand during the playing of "The Star-Spangled Banner." George Foreman, winner of the heavyweight boxing title, celebrated the knockout of his Soviet opponent and protested the protests of his fellow black teammates by waving a small American flag. Politics also swirled around Vera Caslavska, the Czechoslovakian gymnast who overwhelmed Soviet rivals, winning four gold medals and two silvers, after publicly siding with anti-Soviet rebels during the Prague Spring revolt earlier in the year.

The rarefied air at Mexico City's 7,349-foot altitude caused protests of a different sort. Long-distance runners from the high mountains of East Africa did very well, while their low-altitude counterparts suffered—and complained. Of course, the field athletes—the heavers and the jumpers—were delighted. The thin mountain air helped the discuses, and also aided what some have labeled "the greatest single athletic achievement of all time"— Bob Beamon's monumental long jump of 29' 2½" that broke the world record by 1' 9¾" and stood for 23 years. After the jump, the scoreboard flashed 8.9 meters. Puzzled, Beamon asked a teammate how far it was in feet. The man said quietly, "Bob, you jumped 29 feet," and Beamon fell to the ground, weeping.

Many people predicted at the time that his jump would never be bettered. Indeed, Beamon himself never came within two feet, but it finally fell on August 30, 1991, when America's Mike Powell sailed 29' 4". Graciously, Beamon shrugged and said, "Mine was a jump way before its time. It almost made it into the 21st century."

Bettmann/Corbis

It was believed at the time that man could not fly, nor could he jump 29 feet. Soaring over the long-jump pit, **Bob Beamon** quarrels with these physical laws, then is overcome by his feat. The leap had superhuman overtones in that the long-jump record had advanced in such small increments over the years. In 1901 an Irishman jumped 24' 11 3/4"—a new record by a mere four inches. His mark stood for 20 years, until an American extended it by 3 1/4". It climbed gradually until 1935 when Jesse Owens jumped 26' 8 1/4". That was six inches beyond the extant record, and good enough to last for 25 years. In breaking a world record coheld by teammate Ralph Boston and Soviet Igor Ter-Ovanesyan by nearly two feet, Beamon did the impossible.

Jerry Cooke

Michael Rougier

Rich Clarkson/Sports Illustrated

Over 200, 400 and 800 meters in the pool, one woman—girl, rather, at 16—came to Mexico City a clear favorite: **Debbie Meyer**, who had set a world record for each distance at the U.S. Olympic trials. In the Games, she settled for three Olympic records and the knowledge she was the first swimmer to win three individual golds in one Olympics. A schoolteacher from California, **Bill Toomey**, also set an Olympic record—in the decathlon. **Vera Caslavska**, who, like Emil Zatopek, had signed the anti-Soviet 2000-Word Manifesto earlier in the year, won the women's all-around (Russians took second and third), three more golds and two silvers. She then celebrated by getting married in Mexico. Back home, the people loved her, the government did not—and made sure that she remained unemployed.

1972 *Munich*

August 26 to September 10
5,848 men, **1,299** women, **122** countries
U.S.S.R. **99** medals (**50** gold)
U.S.A. **94** medals (**33** gold)
East Germany **66** medals (**20** gold)
West Germany **40** medals (**13** gold)

The fierce politics of the Middle East brought murder to the Olympics. At dawn on the 11th day of competition, Palestinian terrorists took 11 Israeli athletes hostage in the Olympic Village, and killed two there. The other nine died later, along with five terrorists, during a police attack at an airport. A conflict arose over whether the IOC should cancel events. Pressed by President Avery Brundage, members voted to let the Games continue.

Despite the clouds of grief and fear that hung over Munich, these Olympics produced inspiring moments. There was Lasse Viren, a stoic Finnish village policeman, winning gold medals in both the 5,000- and 10,000-meter runs, a glorious double he would repeat four years later in Montreal. There was the black-browed, massive-bellied Soviet weightlifter Vassily Alexeyev, and there was Alexeyev's teammate and physical opposite, the wispy pixie, Olga Korbut, a 4' 11", 85-lb gymnast. Korbut, 17, fell off the uneven bars during the all-around competition, finished a crushing seventh and rushed to her seat in sobs. A day later, she won two golds and a silver in the individual events—and captured the hearts of millions of American women who became hooked on gymnastics.

Despite the presence of so many stars, no athlete dominated like Mark Spitz, 22, the American swimmer who won seven gold medals—more than any other athlete in any sport, ever. More amazingly, he broke the world record in each event. Spitz was a cocky hero, relentless in his pursuit of profit after Munich. "It's like a game to see how much money I can make," he said. "I thought maybe I'd make $20,000, enough to pay my way through dental school. But I guess I've caught on as a symbol or something." He had, and his mega-success—$5 million in the year after the Games—symbolized what a modern Olympic hero meant to Madison Avenue.

To many, especially to Americans, it seemed Mark Spitz was alone in the pool, what with his humongous leads and the inordinate attention he commanded. But that was not the case. In the year prior to the Games, Australian Shane Gould (above) had set five freestyle world records in distances from 100 to 1,500 meters. In Munich she won three golds, a silver and a bronze. In 1973, at 16 years old, she retired.

Co Rentmeester (2)

The exuberance brought to the stage by such as gymnast **Olga Korbut**, seen here in the floor exercises, and veteran Kenyan miler **Kip Keino**, positively flying in the steeplechase, represented the only available antidote to the horrors wrought by the **Black September terrorists**. Keino had held off Jim Ryun in the 1,500 meters in 1968, had finished second over 5,000 meters that year and had added another silver in the 1,500 at Munich. A friend challenged him to enter the steeplechase, a 3,000-meter run with 28 three-foot-high hurdles and seven water jumps. Keino had no experience in the event, and admitted to running it "like an animal." But he called the hurdles "fun," and certainly enjoyed claiming another gold medal.

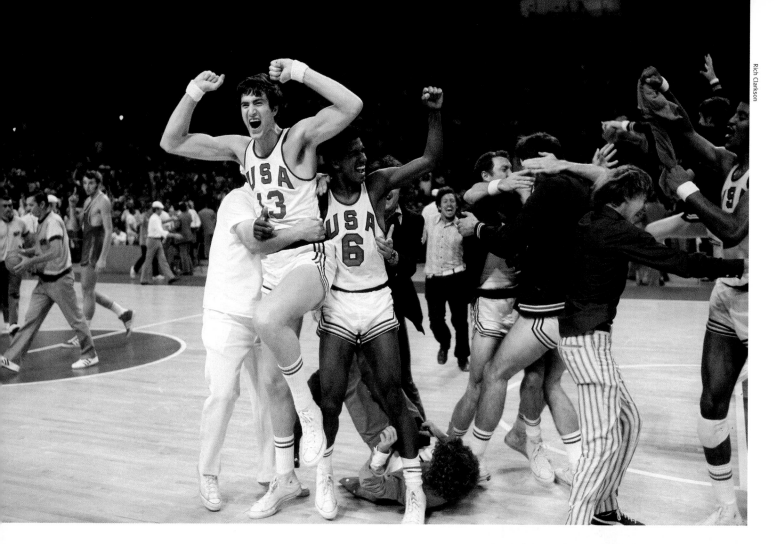

Basketball had long belonged to America, and the U.S. entered the **gold medal game** versus the U.S.S.R. with a record of 62–0 in the Olympics, dating back to 1936. The U.S. took the lead, 50–49, only at game's end. After the clock runs out, the U.S. team celebrates (above). But an official ordered three seconds restored, saying that a Soviet coach had called a timeout. With a second chance, Sasha Belov scored. Now the United States hoopsters are in shock and tears, while the **Soviets** are in ecstasy.

The Olympics has seen few stars who were bigger—all senses of the word—than Soviet superheavyweight weightlifter **Vassily Alexeyev**, 30 years old and 337 pounds when he set four Olympic records at Munich. (He would be 34 and 345 when he set a world and two Olympic records four years later in Montreal.) In the marathon, **Frank Shorter**, a Yale grad who had already finished fifth in the 10,000 meters, grew restless with a slow pace and left the field behind halfway through the race. He entered the stadium to a shower of boos directed at a faker who had taken a "victory" lap before Shorter appeared. But Shorter had no idea, and his dismay was evident. Finally, all is clear, and a smile beams forth.

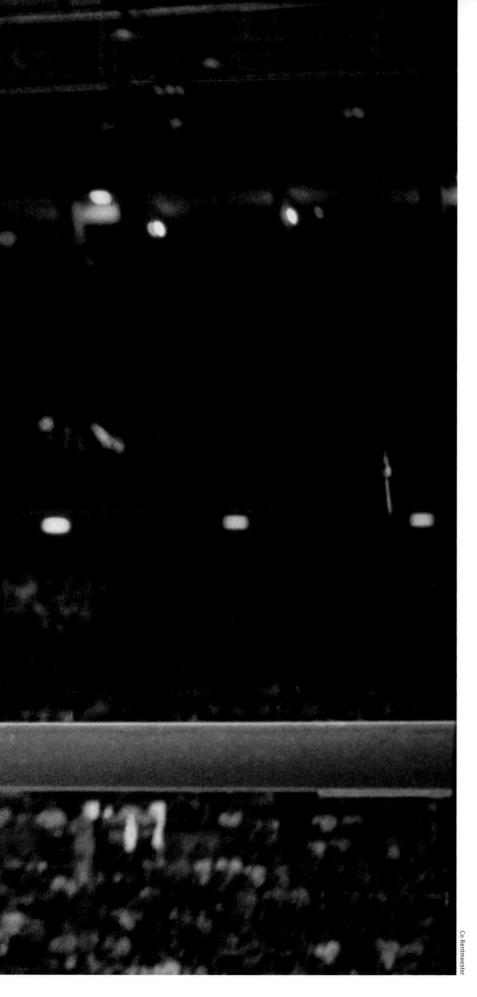

1976 *Montreal*

July 17 to August 1
4,834 men, **1,251** women, **92** countries
U.S.S.R. 125 medals (**49** gold)
U.S.A. 94 medals (**34** gold)
East Germany 90 medals (**40** gold)
Canada 11 medals (**0** gold)

When Montreal bid for the Games, jaunty Mayor Jean Drapeau declared, "The Olympics should not come as an astronomical enterprise. We promise that in Canada, in Montreal, we will present the Games in the true spirit of Olympism, very humble, with simplicity and dignity." Drapeau's original estimate was $120 million, which wouldn't cost taxpayers "one penny." The price came to almost $1.27 billion, which resulted in a paralyzing public debt.

Measured by the athletic performances, however, the investment was solid. All-American boy Bruce Jenner won the decathlon and became an endorsement star. In contrast to Jenner was Cuba's magnificent superheavyweight boxer, Teófilo Stevenson, who won the second of three Olympic gold medals after rejecting $2 million to turn pro.

And then, of course, there was the Romanian waif, Nadia Comaneci, who scored the first perfect 10 in Olympic gymnastic history. With seven 10s in all, she won gold medals in the all-around, uneven bars and balance beam (left). Though her performances pulsed with reckless vitality, Nadia was brooding and impassive when not competing. Was she always sad? "I can smile. But I don't care to." Did she ever cry? "I never cry." What did she think of her perfect 10s? "If it was perfect, I deserved it." What of her Soviet rival who had electrified Munich in '72? "Olga Korbut is just another gymnast."

Nadia returned to Romania, a queen at 14, but trouble dogged her. There was an attempted suicide, huge weight gains and, after she won two golds and two silvers in 1980, a love affair with the abusive son of Romanian dictator Nikolae Ceausescu. She was a guest at L.A. in '84, but she says the Ceausescus refused to let her attend in '88.

In 1989, Nadia made a dramatic escape across the border into Hungary and fled to the U.S. In 1996 she married 1984 American gold medal gymnast Bart Conner. They settled in Norman, Okla.

Co Rentmeester

In the 5,000- and 10,000-meter runs, **Lasse Viren** took the gold, thereby becoming the first to win these in successive Games. Although his times were excellent, the absence of boycotting African nations clearly diluted the field.

After his impressively confident, controlled performance in the decathlon, **Bruce Jenner** and his wife, Chrystie, became ubiquitous media personalities. She had been immensely supportive of him, and he was the first to credit her. Regrettably, they would later divorce. Cuba's **Alberto Juantorena** proved a formidable runner as he became the first to double in both the 400 meters (below) and the 800 meters. The big man combined power, grace and fluidity. Belgian runner Ivo van Damme finished second to Juantorena in the 800. He would die in a car crash that December.

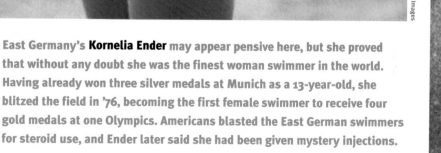

East Germany's **Kornelia Ender** may appear pensive here, but she proved that without any doubt she was the finest woman swimmer in the world. Having already won three silver medals at Munich as a 13-year-old, she blitzed the field in '76, becoming the first female swimmer to receive four gold medals at one Olympics. Americans blasted the East German swimmers for steroid use, and Ender later said she had been given mystery injections.

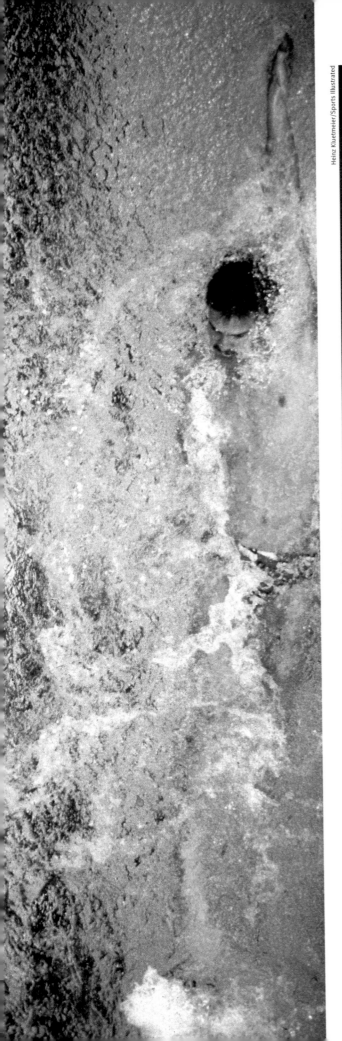

Heinz Kluetmeier/Sports Illustrated

At left, **John Naber** is a model of symmetry as he glides to a world record in the 200-meter backstroke. The 6' 6'' Naber also won the 100-meter race, and took two more golds in relay events. Above, Italian **Klaus Dibiasi** displays the flawless technique that permitted him to win the platform dive for a record third consecutive Games. He also won a silver way back in 1964. His father, Carlo, who served as his coach, competed in the 1936 Olympics.

Heinz Kluetmeier/Sports Illustrated (2)

1980 *Moscow*

July 19 to August 3
4,265 men, **1,088** women, **81** countries
U.S.S.R. **195** medals (**80** gold)
East Germany **126** medals (**47** gold)
Bulgaria **41** medals (**8** gold)

President Jimmy Carter ordered the American boycott of the Moscow Games in retaliation for the Soviet Union's invasion of Afghanistan in 1979. No fewer than 65 countries stayed away, but many athletes felt they had been sacrificed to political expediency. Edwin Moses, history's greatest 400-meter hurdler, said hopelessly, "These are *our* Games."

The Soviets tried to smile through their anger. The Opening Ceremony was particularly cheery, filled with falling rose petals, flying doves of peace and cavorting children in cute bear suits. This went largely unnoticed in the U.S., however, because NBC canceled its coverage of the Games. Also unseen in the States was the ugly behavior of Soviet spectators, who booed and whistled at almost every athlete except their own. They howled so much during the gold-medal pole vault of Poland's Wladyslaw Kozakiewicz that he leaped from the landing pit after his winning jump and answered his detractors with a forceful, obscene gesture.

Soviet athletes hardly needed the boorish support. Led by a pair of handsome gymnasts, they won more medals, 195, than any nation before. Alexander Dityatin earned eight by himself, more than any individual had in any previous Games. "I proved to the world I was the best gymnast on the planet at the time," he said later. "It was a great feeling." His performance in his home-country Olympics won him more than just medals: "I was given money enough to buy a luxurious Volga car. As an Olympic champion I did not have to stand in the three-to-five years' long line for an apartment in Leningrad. Also I was elected a deputy of the City Council."

In complement to Dityatin's performance, the veteran Nikolai Andrianov won two gold, two silver and a bronze to add to his trove from Munich (one gold, one silver, one bronze) and Montreal (four gold, two silver, one bronze). These combined performances made Andrianov the Olympics' all-time male individual medal winner with 15.

Tit for tat: Great Brits **Sebastian Coe** (No. 254 in both photos) and **Steve Ovett** (279) unfortunately found themselves at the top of their middle-distance careers at the same time. It was believed coming into the Games that Coe had the advantage over 800 meters and Ovett had a distinct edge at 1,500. When Ovett nipped world-record holder Coe in the 800 (opposite), it was generally felt that Coe would return to England winless, especially as Ovett owned part of the world record in the 1,500 and a three-year, 42-race win streak in the mile and 1,500. But Coe came through. He again won the 1,500 and took silver in the 800 in 1984.

The statistics tell a story of Soviet might: **Alexander Dityatin** won three golds (including one on the rings, left), four silvers and a bronze, and scored the first-ever 10 by a male gymnast with one of his long horse vaults. Finishing second to him in the all-around was the veteran and defending champion **Nikolai Andrianov**, who also won two golds, another silver and a bronze (on the horizontal bar, opposite). This brought Andrianov's career total to 15—seven golds among them—the most ever won by a male, but not any, Olympian. Another Soviet gymnast, Larysa Latynina, had won 18 medals from 1956 to '64.

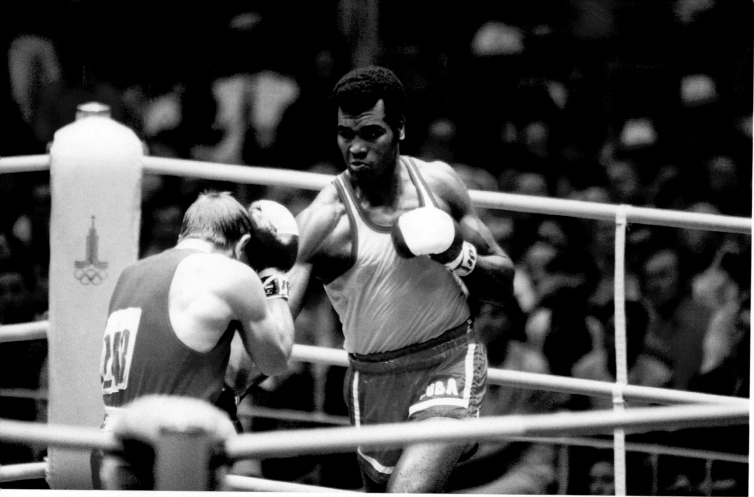

Superheavyweight boxer **Teófilo Stevenson** of Cuba had the most sterling—well, golden—amateur career ever, winning Olympic titles in 1972, '76 and, here, in '80. **Nadia Comaneci** glowers as coach **Bela Karolyi** erupts when questionable judging costs her the all-around title. She won two more golds in the beam and floor exercises. U.S.S.R. swim czar **Vladimir Salnikov**, who had trained in the U.S., won three golds and set a world mark in the 1,500.

The 3,000 Poles in attendance were no match for a sea of Soviets, who jeered every successful attempt—and there were plenty—by pole-vaulter **Wladyslaw Kozakiewicz**. He secured the gold medal without missing once, then set his sights higher—on a world record. He got it on his second try, clearing 18' 11 ½". Above: Since the crowd has let Kozakiewicz know what they think of him, he returns the favor.

The saga begins. Cases can be made for Thorpe, Didrikson, Nurmi, Owens, Zatopek, Oerter, Latynina, Viren, Spitz—even such as Ewry, undisputed king of discontinued track and field events. The arguments would involve one shining moment, extraordinary durability or the ability to come through. But any discussion of the greatest Olympic athlete ever starts with Alabaman Carl Lewis, King Carl, a mere princeling at 23 in L.A. when he surged to an eight-foot margin in the 100-meter final, set an Olympic record—at low altitude—in the 200, won his first of four Olympic long jumps, and finally (here) anchors the world-record-breaking 4x100 U.S. relay team.

1984 *Los Angeles*

July 28 to August 12
5,458 men, **1,620** women, **141** nations
U.S.A. **177** medals (**83** gold)
Romania **53** medals (**20** gold)

American stars abounded, not least since a Soviet-bloc boycott—a reciprocal gesture after the U.S. strike in 1980—left the L.A. Games bereft of many of the world's best athletes. Edwin Moses won the 400-meter hurdles by extending a winning streak that had begun in the summer of 1977—102 victories through L.A. and 107 in all before it would end in 1987. And joyful young Carl Lewis began his triumphant Olympic run by replicating Jesse Owens's feat of four track-and-field golds.

Unlike Moses and Lewis, gymnast Mary Lou Retton was something of a surprise. At 16, she was only four foot nine, 95 pounds, wore a size 1 dress and size 3 shoes, but her boundless effervescence made her appear far larger. She won only one gold medal, but it was for the women's all-around, and it came after a perfect last-chance execution of a full-twisting layout Tsukahara vault that was accompanied by her gleeful shout, "I stuck it!"

No athlete was more dazzling than diver Greg Louganis. He had competed as a callow, frightened 16-year-old in Montreal and won silver in the platform event, then had missed his shot at two golds in Moscow. In L.A., he won the springboard and platform, becoming the first male to break 700 points in both events. Louganis's good looks and wholesome smile made him seem the ideal American boy. In fact, he was a troubled young man, living with an abusive gay lover. Early in 1988, he learned he was HIV positive, and he competed in Seoul under a horrendous cloud of secrecy and fear. "I was in a total panic that I might cause someone harm," he wrote in his memoir *Breaking the Surface*. Improbably, Louganis did cut his head when he struck the springboard during a difficult dive, but the harm was only to himself. He recovered and went on to win both events in Seoul, becoming the only male diver to win four Olympic gold medals.

Louganis gave up competing after Seoul and became a competent actor. He is also a spokesman in AIDS fund-raising and education campaigns.

John Zimmerman

John Zimmerman

Walter Iooss Jr./Sports Illustrated

Images of perfection: Against a blue L.A. sky, **Greg Louganis** is the embodiment of the Olympic athletic ideal, a Greek god (well, actually of Samoan-European ancestry) floating free of earthly constraints. In the modern Olympic tradition of tinier-than-thou women gymnasts, **Mary Lou Retton** follows Olga and Nadia into the hearts and minds of aspirant little girls everywhere by sticking her Tsukahara. **Edwin Moses** set a world record in winning the 400-meter hurdles in Montreal in 1976. In 1980, his latest world record was more than a second and a half faster than the winning time in Moscow. Here, he leads start to finish in L.A. In 1988, still the world-record holder, he would add a bronze. He was the ultimate hurdler.

Neil Leifer

It had been a long road back for female distance runners after the Olympics booted the 800 meters out of the Games following its first appearance in 1928. (That race returned in 1960.) In 1984, the promised land was reached as the women's marathon debuted. Maine's **Joan Benoit** (left) waltzed away from Norway's Grete Waitz and won in a walk. The most riveting final lap in the stadium belonged to **Gabriele Andersen-Scheiss**. The Swiss runner had been overcome by the hot sun and, in the stadium, took nearly six minutes to hobble to the finish line in 37th place, TV cameras capturing the agony. Fortunately, her ordeal did not prompt officials to reconsider the women's marathon's place in the Games.

The legacy of Wilma Rudolph and Wyomia Tyus fell in L.A. to **Evelyn Ashford**, 27, tearful after winning the 100 meters in Olympic record time. British decathlete **Daley Thompson** repeats as champ: a boycott double. U.S. middle-distance queen **Mary Decker** howls after tangling with Zola Budd and tripping in the 3,000.

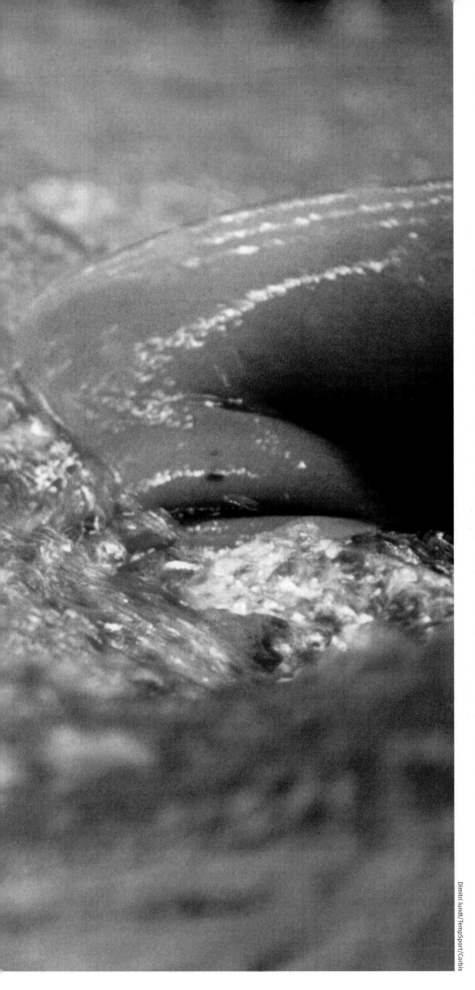

1988 *Seoul*

September 17 to October 2
6,983 men, **2,438** women, **160** countries
U.S.S.R. **132** medals (**55** gold)
East Germany **102** medals (**37** gold)
U.S.A. **94** medals (**36** gold)
South Korea **33** medals (**12** gold)

There was much to celebrate in Seoul, particularly an IOC decision to drop the outmoded requirement that all competitors be "amateur." This opened the door to such exciting events as Steffi Graf defeating Gabriela Sabatini for the gold in tennis. It also did away with a lot of hypocrisy among athletes, who had been forced to lie about their financial status in order to remain eligible for the Games.

Though no one knew it at the time, the Seoul Games were the last in which the powerhouse East German team would compete as an entity. Thus, it was fitting that one of the top athletes here was a statuesque (6' ¾") young woman from East Germany. Kristin Otto (left), 22, won six gold medals in swimming—more in a single Olympics than any other woman. And she won them in three different styles—freestyle, backstroke and butterfly—something no one (not Weissmuller, not Spitz) had done.

Otto retired after Seoul and returned to Berlin to participate in demonstrations that led to the fall of the Berlin Wall in 1989. Crumbling with it was the athletic juggernaut that communism had built. It was commonplace during the '90s for former East German coaches to make headlines—and deutsche marks—by confessing to illegal coaching practices, such as feeding steroids to their athletes, often without their knowledge. Otto was infuriated by the notion that she had been beefed up by steroids and had not deserved her triumphs: "I get very angry when athletes bear the burden," she said. "No one can take my success at Seoul away from me. I was like Mark Spitz, lucky to have a great gift, and those six medals were the result of many years' work."

The medal won in Seoul by Canadian Ben Johnson over Carl Lewis in the 100-meter dash was unquestionably the result of a steroids-enhanced performance. After testing positive for the drugs, Johnson forfeited his gold in one of the most notorious scandals in the annals of sport.

In the 100-meter final, Canadian **Ben Johnson** was the class of the field, besting even Carl Lewis (center) while setting a world record. Three days later, Johnson was revealed to be nothing but a classless cheat who had resorted to steroids. At left, he is homeward bound after his record was annulled and his medal given to Lewis. **Florence Griffith Joyner** emerged from the mean streets of Watts, Calif., to taste gold in the 100 meters (opposite), 200 meters (world record) and the 4x100 relay. The sudden success of "Flojo" was something of a surprise, as she had previously been sort of an also-ran. The whiff of steroid use lingered about her until her sudden death in 1998 at age 38.

She wasn't too big, and she had a rather strange stroke, but she sure knew how to get from one end of the pool to the other. Seventeen-year-old **Janet Evans** won the 400-meter medley, broke her own world record in the 400-meter freestyle and also took gold in the 800 freestyle. She would repeat her win in the 800 freestyle in Barcelona. Astonishingly, her world records in the 400, 800 and 1,500, set in 1988 and '89, were still standing at the onset of Olympic Year 2004. It was scary when **Greg Louganis** cracked his head in a late qualifying dive. However, he would come back a half hour later to qualify, and he went on to take his second-straight gold in the springboard. **Sergei Bubka** was a huge favorite in the pole vault, but he cleared on only one attempt, his final, to take the gold. The peerless Soviet would set 35 world records.

1992 *Barcelona*

July 25 to August 9
7,108 men, **2,851** women, **172** countries
U.S.A. **108** medals (**37** gold)
Unified Team **102** medals (**45** gold)
Germany **82** medals (**33** gold)
Spain **22** medals (**13** gold)

The Barcelona Games were as beautiful and joyous as any in history. In the space of a single four-year Olympiad, the world had become a comparative Elysian land of peace and sweetness. For the first time in 40 years, the Summer Games were played without East-West hostilities poisoning the air. There were no boycotts for the first time in 20 years. No athletes performed as surrogate cold warriors, no white hats, no black hats. The Berlin Wall was gone, and the Germanys marched together. The monolithic Soviet Union had been fractured into a dozen independent, democratic countries. Although they competed together as the Unified Team in Barcelona, they couldn't wait to go their own ways.

The world's No. 1 pariah nation, South Africa, was back in an Olympics for the first time in 32 years because the evil of apartheid was on the way out. Professional athletes were not only welcomed, they were also lionized—most famously in the case of the U.S. "Dream Team" of pro basketball stars.

And still, one athlete stood out here as particularly deserving of her triumph. Jackie Joyner-Kersee (right) was born to deep poverty in 1962 in East St. Louis, Ill. She was named after Jacqueline Kennedy; her grandmother declared at her birth, "Someday this girl will be the first lady of something." She won a scholarship to UCLA for basketball, met her future husband and track coach, Bob Kersee, and, despite recurring injuries and crippling attacks of asthma, she reigned for a decade over one of sport's most demanding events, the heptathlon. By 1992 she had already won the world championship twice, as well as a gold medal in Seoul and a silver in L.A. She also had been the world long-jump champ twice and had won Olympic gold in that event in '88. Now she successfully defended her heptathlon title and took silver in the jump. Bruce Jenner, the '76 decathlon winner, declared her "the greatest multi-event athlete ever, man or woman."

George Tiedemann/Sports Illustrated

With Carl Lewis out because he was ill during the U.S. trials, the way was open for **Linford Christie** (left) in the 100 meters. As fellow Briton **Derek Redmond** (near right) settled into the blocks for a semifinal in the 400, he dedicated the race to his father, **Jim**. Some 150 meters into the race, he fell, then tried to hobble. Jim came down from the stands and helped his son reach the finish line—truly a finish for the ages.

The women's 100-meter dash ended with the closest finish, men's or women's, ever at that distance in the Olympics. The fifth-place runner came in less than a 10th of a second behind the winner, **Gail Devers** (second from right), who had overcome a long bout earlier in her career with one bizarre ailment after another. At the 1991 world championships, **Mike Powell** had jumped 29' 4 ½", finally besting Bob Beamon's historic 1968 leap. At Barcelona, though, Powell got off to a poor start, and ended up taking silver to Carl Lewis's gold. Powell would go on, however, to win 34 consecutive long-jump events, including the 1993 world championships.

Thirteen-year-old **Fu Mingxia** had been removed from her home in Wuhan at nine and taken to a diving school in Beijing, where she was subjected to unthinkable methods of training. To help protect children, rules were established that divers be at least 14 in the year of the Games. She turned 14 three weeks after completely dominating the platform event. In 1996 she would win on both the platform and the springboard. At right, the Unified Team's **Vitaly Scherbo** demonstrates the control he exercised in winning the all-around gymnastics crown. The 20-year-old from Minsk would become the first gymnast to win six gold medals in one Olympics.

John McDonough/Sports Illustrated

Santiago Lyon/AP Wide World

Easily the finest assemblage of hoopsters ever to compete in the Olympics, the Dream Team was led by **Magic Johnson** and featured such immortals as Larry Bird and Michael Jordan. The coach, Chuck Daly, never called a timeout for the entire Games.

Peter Read Miller/Sports Illustrated

1996 *Atlanta*

July 19 to August 4
6,806 men, **3,512** women, **197** countries
U.S.A. **101** medals (**44** gold)
Germany **65** medals (**20** gold)
Russian Federation **63** medals (**26** gold)
China **50** medals (**16** gold)

Terrorism returned to the Games when a bomb exploded at Centennial Olympic Park, killing one and injuring 110. (In May 2003, Eric Robert Rudolph was arrested, and remains under indictment.) Inside the arena, American Michael Johnson and Marie-José Pérec of France both won the 200 and the 400 meters, which had never been done in an unboycotted Olympics. Briton Steve Redgrave won the coxless pairs in rowing, the first in his sport to earn a gold in four Games. But one flamboyant figure, in his Olympic swan song, stole the limelight.

F. Carlton Lewis, having won eight gold medals through the Barcelona Games, was one of the Olympics' major icons, yet shadows had played across his career. In L.A., spectators booed him because he refused to try for a world record in his last four long jumps, choosing to save himself for coming events. In '88, Ben Johnson's disqualification gave Lewis a gold in the 100 meters, but other failures cost him two more: After going undefeated for almost two years, he finished second in the 200 meters to his training partner; and a teammate's botched handoff in the 4x100 kept him from another victory. In the trials for Barcelona, a virus kept him from qualifying for the team in the 100- and 200-meter individual races. Still, Lewis anchored the 4x100 relay, taking the baton with a one-meter lead and increasing the victory margin to seven meters. He added a gold in the long jump, defeating world-record holder Mike Powell by 1' ¼".

In Atlanta, again competing in the long jump, Lewis was finally a sentimental favorite—though barely rated a contender. But with 82,000 cheering him, he leaped 27' 10 ¾", his best jump at sea level in four years. He became the third person in Olympic history to win the same individual event four times, the fourth (after Nurmi, Latynina and Spitz) to earn nine career golds and, in the eyes of many, the greatest Olympian of the century.

After winning as an 18-year-old at the 1960 Games, Cassius Clay went nowhere without his gold medal—not to bed, not to breakfast. Then, back in Louisville, there were some ugly racial incidents, and he threw the medal away. "Whatever illusions I'd built up in Rome as the All-American Boy were gone." Many years later, **Muhammad Ali** returns, this time as a beloved hero for good. Opposite, **Carl Lewis** doesn't look as young as he did when he first burst onto the scene, but he can still jump farther than anyone else here.

Walter Iooss Jr./Sports Illustrated

He had been the best 200- and 400-meter man in the world since the year 1990. He lost in the semifinals at Barcelona because of food poisoning. This time around, nothing would stop **Michael Johnson**. He broke his own world record in the 200 (opposite, in his trademark upright style) and also went gold by the largest margin since 1896 in the 400, which he again won at the 2000 Games. A native of Guadeloupe, **Marie-José Pérec** moved to Paris at age 16. Leading up to the 1992 Olympics, she had become an obsession with the press in her new country, and she validated their interest when she won the gold in the 400 meters. Everyone in '96 had been anticipating Johnson's 200-400 double, but the shared feat by Pérec gave Atlanta a real double-dip.

In a dramatic semifinal match between longtime rivals, Norway's **Gro Espeseth** and **Mia Hamm** of the U.S. give it all they've got. The U.S. side won, and went on to take the first women's soccer gold medal. In a matter of moments, 87-pound **Kerri Strug** was transported from just another gymnast to a national treasure. The U.S was leading in the team combined exercises, but could require Strug to stick a vault. However, she fell and badly hurt her ankle. She told coach **Bela Karolyi** she couldn't go again. He replied, "We need a 9.6." Of course, she hit a 9.712, and wearing a soft cast, she is carried to the medals stand by her coach. At left, the scene at **Centennial Olympic Park**.

With the Opera House in the background, the inaugural triathlon and the Sydney Games are off with a splash.

2000 *Sydney*

September 15 to October 1
6,582 men, **4,069** women, **199** countries
U.S.A. **97** medals (**40** gold)
Russian Federation **88** medals (**32** gold)
China **59** medals (**28** gold)
Australia **58** medals (**16** gold)

The glittering Sydney Games illustrated just how far de Coubertin's concept had come in its 24 iterations (plus 18 winter editions). Consider: At Sydney, 16,033 members of the media delivered the must-have news. The stories they told were mostly of heroes, though there were a few villains. U.S. shot-putter C.J. Hunter, husband of celebrated track star Marion Jones, was disgraced in a steroids scandal, as performance-enhancing drugs continued to blight modern sport. Jones, for her part, was stoic, and performed wonderfully, winning the 100 meters and 200 meters easily, a third gold in the 4x400 and a bronze in both the long jump and the 4x100-meter relay. The star of the pool was hometown boy Ian Thorpe, the Thorpedo. A rosy-cheeked lad of 17 propelled by world-class size-17 feet, he won three golds and two silvers, setting a world record in the 400-meter freestyle. As a wizened veteran in 2004, he is set to duel for top honors in Athens with the latest teenage phenom, Michael Phelps of the U.S.

Michael Johnson and rower Steve Redgrave extended their Olympic legacies, but the most electrifying moment of the Games—and one of the most emotional in the history of the Olympic movement—belonged to Australian runner Cathy Freeman. Under enormous pressure—running with nothing less than a continent on her shoulders—she prevailed over 400 meters in 49.11 thrilling seconds, then collapsed on the track, overcome, as thunderous applause rained upon her. Why the tumult? Freeman is an Aborigine, and Aborigines, the indigenous people of Australia, had been persecuted in their homeland for most of the previous two centuries. In the run-up to the Games, most Australians, seizing on the new millennium as a time to confront their past, pointed to Cathy as a symbol. When she came through, they—and, somewhere, de Coubertin—cheered and cheered.

Eric Feterberg/AFP/Getty Images

In 1996, **Cathy Freeman** (left and below) became the first Aborigine to take home an individual medal when she won the silver in the 400 meters. This time around, she had been selected to light the cauldron to start the Games; she was expected to win. A lot of pressure, but she showed she could handle it, as she finished first in the 400, dropped to the ground to gather her senses and then bore the flags of Australia and the Aborigines on her victory lap.

An injury kept her out of the action at Atlanta, which only served to ensure that **Marion Jones** (above, in the 100 meters) would unleash her full fury on Sydney. She destroyed the field in the 100, cruised to gold in the 200 and added another first in the 4x400 meters. With the addition of two bronzes, Jones became the first woman to win five gold medals in athletics in the same Olympics. **Konstadinos Kenteris** was all but invisible before the race, but when the 200 meters was in the books, he was the one with the gold. It marked the first time that a Greek man had won a gold medal in a running event since the marathon was held at the first modern Games back in 1896.

Bob Martin/Sports Illustrated; top: Frakes/Callow

Australia, a continent of swimmers and surfers, likes its heroes wet: Fraser, Rose, Gould and Kieren Perkins—who won the 1,500 in Barcelona and Atlanta, then finished second to Aussie Grant Hackett in Sydney. Therefore, enormous pressure sat upon the broad shoulders of Sydneysider **Ian Thorpe**, who was preternaturally calm through the storm. In one of the hugest upsets of the Games, Greco-Roman legend **Alexander Karelin**, the giant from Siberia who hadn't lost a match in 13 years, made a mistake and was beaten 1–0 by **Rulon Gardner** of Wyoming, who is head-over-heels happy with his victory.

Joe McNally

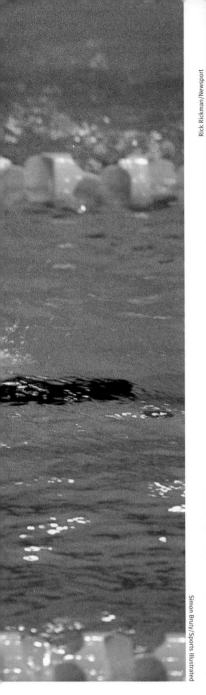

In the inaugural holding of the women's pole-vault event, 31-year-old **Stacy Dragila** came out on top. But this isn't surprising, since the native of Auburn, Calif., has had a career of firsts. What might surprise, though, is that she is nicknamed the Goat Roper, after her skill in the rodeo event in which a rider lassos and trusses a goat.

2004 *Athens*

August 13 to August 29
10,500 athletes, **201** countries
Competition in **28** sports
Estimated cost **more than $5.6 billion**

The long Olympic road from Athens to Athens turned bumpy near its end, as delays and cost over-runs made sports fans and government officials fretful. The swimming pool, which was to have a roof, will now have no roof. Coaches are packing extra sunscreen, and have been scouting spots around the deck where their athletes might catch some shade.

But pre-Games tension has attended other recent Olympics, as the spectacles have become ever larger and more complicated to stage. It is a developing Olympic tradition for the host city to rally, get the nails nailed down and the cauldron lit on time. That is the expectation for Athens, 2004.

The eternal flame, for a second time, will have come from just up the road. Although the organizers chose to arrange a world-tour torch relay by plane, train, bike, motorbike and, oh, yes, on foot, they could, had they wanted, have enlisted a couple of middle-distance runners from Olympia High to jog the thing over to Panathinnaiko Stadium.

In the photograph at left, the Olympic flame is kindled on March 25 by the Greek actress Thalia Prokopiou, who is playing the high priestess. She employs the rays of the sun in the sanctuary where the original Games were born 2,780 years ago. Then, on a journey that would boggle modern Olympics founder Baron Pierre de Coubertin—never mind the ancients—the torch is on its way to 33 stops in 26 countries on five continents before returning for a 3,300-mile nationwide tour of Greece. Thus, finally, to Athens.

One thing the baron and the ancients would understand and applaud: Organizers are imploring all humankind to respect Ekechiria—the Olympic Truce—and to cease hostilities during the fortnight. Last year, 190 member-states of the United Nations cosponsored a Greek resolution asking for peace during the Games. Such pleas have gone unheeded in the past, and violence has visited the arena. As the Olympics returns to its birthplace, we shall see. Let the Games begin!